50 Wildlife Hotspots

Grand Teton National Park and Surrounding Communities

A Guide for Photographers and Wildlife Enthusiasts

Moose Henderson

Sastrugi Press

FOREWORD

For a wildlife photographer to consistently produce successful images, preparedness is paramount. Success is often proportionate to due diligence and time spent in the field. It can take days or weeks of researching social media sites, periodicals, and books to learn the prime location and the best time of year to capture species-specific behavior. Landscape photography and environmental conditions can dictate clothing requirements. You get the idea; the more informed you are before setting off on your journey, the greater the chance for success in the field.

With his book *50 Wildlife Hotspots: Grand Teton National Park and Surrounding Communities,* Moose Henderson has provided the wildlife observer and photographer with a concise, wonderfully formatted, and easy to follow and informative tutorial to put you precisely in the right place at the right time for a variety of wildlife and landscape opportunities. Each one of the fifty wildlife hotspot locations provided in the book provides a wealth of wildlife information garnered from Moose's doctorate degree in wildlife biology, an undergraduate degree in geology, and extensive time and observations spent afield.

The *Site Specific Photography Tips* provide recommendations on photographic equipment and technique, enlightening animal behavior, including: their most active time of day, how flighty a species is of your presence, and more. *Directions* to locations are precise, with Moose offering maps, mile(s) to your next turn, and sides of the road that might contain wildlife. *Highlights* provide additional information with regard to animal whereabouts at specific locations and times of the year. *Wildlife In Area* illustrations offers insight into the species most likely to inhabit a specific location.

Whether you are a wildlife photographer, observer, or nature lover, Moose's *50 Wildlife Hotspots: Grand Teton National Park and Surrounding Communities* will ensure you maximize the opportunities present in this beautiful ecosystem.

Good Light and Safe Travels All,
(Chas) Charles Glatzer, M.Photog.
Canon Explorer of Light

INTRODUCTION

Grand Teton National Park and the surrounding area is one of the premier scenic and wildlife sites of the world. It is on the "bucket list" of nearly all that love scenic and wild places. The park consists of approximately 310,000 acres or 480 square miles. The park is accessed by three roads: one from Jackson Hole to the south, second from Yellowstone to the north, and the third from Dubois to the east. Few roads from the outside connect the entire area of Jackson Hole. The park to the north borders it, the Tetons to the west, Hoback and Snake River Canyons to the south, and the mountains to the east. Jackson Hole contains one of the largest concentrations of animals in the lower forty-eight states.

Jackson Hole has a rich history that dates to numerous Native American tribes that hunted and fished the area, followed by the explorers that came west in the late 1800s, soon followed by settlers. Some recognized that the area was so beautiful that it would soon be spoiled by an influx of people. These folks had the foresight to save the area for all to enjoy. Because of this vision, 97% of Teton County is designated as national park, national forest, or other government lands, forever protected to all to enjoy. Many books delve into the history, geology, geography and other aspects of the area. This book focuses on the locations of animals and iconic places for viewing the mountains, lakes, and other attractions.

Few fishermen would argue the value of local knowledge. Locals that are active year-around become in-tune with the rhythm, timing, climate, and movements of an area. In *The Sporting Magazine*, (January 1844) Prince Albert stated that, "in March there requires a good local knowledge of a river to command sport, I know a mile of water which in March never holds a fish…" To get the maximum utility of the Tetons, local knowledge is essential.

Many tourists that visit the area hire a wildlife touring company to show them the area. A quality tour guide has extensive "local knowledge" and they are in-tune with the rhythm of the area. Most of the tour guides are university trained as a biologist or in other scientific fields. However, a wildlife tour is also guided by the speed and pace of the touring company. What if you could do a wildlife tour at your pace? The purpose of this guide is to serve as your "local knowledge" and provides the most probable locations of wildlife during various seasons and months of the year.

Unlike a zoo where the animals are caged and waiting to be seen at any time, animals in the Tetons are free ranging. They are wild animals and finding them can be difficult. However, with the local knowledge provided in this book, you will have the same opportunity to find the animals as the touring companies. However, you will be able to do it on your schedule and according to your timetable.

Park regulations require everyone to remain at least 100 yards from bears and wolves and 25 yards from all other animals. Even if the animal approaches, you are expected to maintain this minimum distance. The risk of a bear or wolf attack is relatively rare. Between 1994 and 2015, bears in Grand Teton National Park attacked only six people and none were fatal. However, in the 142-year history of Yellowstone, eight people have lost their lives to bear attacks. The most recent death was a hiker in Yellowstone in 2015. Photographers are also at risk. A man was killed in 1986 by a sow grizzly near Hayden Valley in Yellowstone. Maintain a safe distance and always carry bear spray; learn the proper use of bear spray before you need it.

Most visitors know to avoid large predators like bears, mountain lions, and wolves. However, even the apparently slow animals are very dangerous. Park records show that bison are responsible for more human-animal interactions than all other animals combined. Bison appear slow and lumbering but they can run at 35mph and leap a six-foot fence. From 2000–2015, twenty-five bison attacks were documented by the park service. Imagine the possible injuries caused by a two thousand pound bison moving as fast as a car.

Attacks by animals are also risky for the animal. Frequently, the animal will be relocated or even eliminated by the park service after an attack. Please do not become a statistic; maintain a safe distance from animals. Even if others are getting too close, protect yourself and your family. No picture is worth the injury from an animal.

Safety

When the animals are nearby, there tend to be volunteer ranger brigade members and park rangers everywhere you look. Nevertheless, you are responsible for your own safety and the safety of your family. Park regulations require a minimum of 25 yards between yourself and any animal and a minimum of 100 yards between yourself and bears and wolves. If the animal approaches, you are required to keep your distance.

Every year, there are a couple unfortunate accidents, usually with bison-human interactions. Deaths are rare but do not become a statistic. You may notice some of the photographers with long lenses getting closer than you feel is safe. It is possible, with years of experience, to learn to read the "body language" of the animals.

Some folks think they can read the animals yet they become part of the accident statistics. Few things can ruin a vacation faster than an extended stay at a hospital. Bear spray is insurance. Always carry it by your side or on your belt. Carrying it in your backpack will do little good, as bear attacks are viciously fast.

Consider the safety of the animals. Give them plenty of room to feed and carry on their daily activities. The elk and moose rut can be a very dangerous time, as cows are avoiding the advances of bulls. It is a shared responsibility of all to protect the wonderful wildlife of Grand Teton. Never approach an animal, their dens, or bird nesting areas. The animals and birds you help protect will be here for the next generation if we all do our part to ensure their survival.

Cameras and Site-Specific Photography Tips

Cameras come in all shapes and sizes. Many folks will visit the park with only a cell phone camera whereas others will use a point-and-shoot, a 35mm camera, or even an 8X10 view camera. All cameras can record your park visit and provide you with years of memories.

Each hotspot or location in this book contains these site-specific photography tips. These tips recommend lenses for specific animals. The lens recommendations are for a full-frame 35mm camera (sensor size of approximately 36×24 mm). Because of safety concerns and access to the animals, many times a telephoto lens of 200mm to 600mm is needed.

Typically, sensors smaller than a full-frame 35mm camera are advertised according to a "magnification factor." Simply multiply your lens size (in millimeters) by the "magnification factor" for your sensor size. For example, if the photo tips section recommends a 600mm lens; a 400mm lens on an APS-sized sensor (approximate 1.5X crop factor) is roughly equivalent to a 600mm lens on a full-frame sensor. It is not a truly magnified image on the sensor, though. Consult your camera manual for a more thorough explanation.

There are also attachment devices marketed for cell phones that magnify the image. These devices clip onto the cell phone and overlie the camera lens. These telephone lenses are designated by magnification factor, such as 4X-12X. The photography tips sections are designed for traditional camera lenses but can be converted to a magnification factor. The human eye is approximately equivalent to a 50mm lens on a full-frame camera. Divide the lens recommendations by 50mm to convert to magnification factors. For example, 100mm=2X, 150mm=3X, 200mm=4X, 300mm=6X, 400mm=8X, 500mm=10X and 600mm=12X.

The Tetons have a definite rhythm; as the year starts, there is abundant deep snow. Toward the end of April, the snow begins to dissipate, and the bears come out from their winter hibernation. Trees, shrubs, and grasses almost explode with their new growth. As summer approaches, temperatures climb into the low to mid-80s and the animals become more difficult to find. The bison rut is typically in the summertime. Temperatures begin to moderate in August and typically the first snow falls in September. The moose and elk rut is during the latter part of September. Snow begins to accumulate in October and the bears begin preparing for their winter siesta. In winter, elk, pronghorn, and bison have migrated from their summer ranges to their winter range, typically in the lowland areas. Bighorn sheep migrate down from the high country as snow accumulates. The rut is near the second week of December. Winter is a time of abundant snowfall (typically 400-600 inches), brutally cold temperatures, difficult road conditions but also fewer tourists. Many of the animals are easier to observe because the deciduous trees are leafless, and the ground is covered with a white blanket of snow.

Itineraries

Animals generally follow set patterns. To view or photograph these animals, it is good to know the best locations to look and best times to be in certain areas. Even the landscapes and flora follow a predictable pattern. Tourist season runs from approximately May through mid-October. A second tourist season, ski season, is from approximately December through March. The following itineraries will give areas to look for animals and the best areas for landscape photography.

January-March: If you are among the few brave and intrepid folks that come to enjoy the Tetons during the dead of winter, you will be treated to brutally cold temperatures, deep snow on and adjacent to the roads, few other tourists, and the most beautiful barren landscapes this side of Siberia. The author spent two years in Siberia. This is not a literary exaggeration. There is a certain beauty in the extremes and the Tetons in winter are just extreme.

Most of the wildlife will be concentrated in the lowland areas of the National Elk Refuge and the Gros Ventre area (hotspots 1-3, 5). Nevertheless, it is always worth a drive north to look for foxes, skunks, coyotes, wolves, and other critters that are braving the deep snow while hunting for the next meal. Generally, animals flee less when they are facing extremes. If you remain in or near your car, most likely a fox or coyote will continue to hunt for voles or mice just twenty yards from the roadside.

Winter is also the time for owls and eagles. Great gray owls and great horned owls are most common in the northern section of Spring Gulch Road and the road headed toward the Swan Ponds (hotspots 46 and 48). Golden and bald eagles are most common on the elk refuge (hotspots 1-2). Occasionally, an elk will die of old age, exposure, or wolf predation. An elk carcass is nearly seven hundred pounds of frozen food and the animals take turns feeding on the remains. Generally, the wolves have first rights and they feed at night or very early in the day. The coyotes and eagles generally follow the wolves. Add in a few crows and ravens to the mix and you have a very active carcass.

Suggested January-March Itinerary: During this time frame, you can generally sleep later as the sun will not rise until after eight and will generally set near five in the afternoon. It can be difficult to find animals in the dead of winter. Of course, there are plenty at the National Elk Refuge (hotspots 1-5). At first light, take some images at Snake River Overlook or maybe Oxbow Bend (hotspots 18 and 22). Maybe run up to Colter Bay and look where the ice fishing huts are on the lake. Many times you can find foxes in this area trying to steal a fish (hotspot 32).

Moose are elusive during this time because of the extreme shortage of material to eat. They are concentrated in the river bottom of the Gros Ventre. The Gros Ventre extends into the area near Spring Gulch Road, so moose are occasionally on the roadside feeding on deciduous twigs of the cottonwoods, aspen, and willows (hotspot 46). Mule deer will be seen near the town of Kelly on nearly a daily basis (hotspots 9 and 11). In fact, drive through the town of Kelly as some of the deer "steal" food from the livestock. Patrol the northern stretch of Spring Gulch Road and the road near the Swan Ponds for owls (hotspots 46 and 48).

In years past, the lower Gros Ventre wolf pack has had a den to the north of Mailbox Corner (hotspot 14). It is a rare sight to see a wolf but certainly a thrill that will seldom be topped. This area is always worth a drive on the chance that the wolves are active. Do not leave the roadside and do not venture into the area near the cabins. Winter is a stressful time for animals and they need to conserve their energy. Always consider the welfare of the animals first.

April: Snow begins to melt in mid-April and the bears begin to appear from hibernation. Bears will be concentrated in the northern areas of the park. Typically, only boars and sows without cubs will be out in mid-April. Areas of Pilgrim Creek, Pacific Creek, Willow Flats, Oxbow Bend, and Elk Flats (hotspots 30, 25, 29, 27 and 21) are the prime areas of the park for bears in April. The highway between Moran Junction and Togwotee Pass (hotspot 22) is also a prime location for grizzly bears. The bears forage along the highway in the meadows for dandelions.

Bison and elk begin the slow migration from their winter range on the National Elk Refuge (hotspot 5) toward their summer range further north. Elk and bison will be concentrated in the Gros Ventre area (hotspots 7-11), near the town of Kelly (hotspot 9), and near the highway from the National Elk Refuge to Elk Flats (hotspots 5 and 21). Moose will be found in the bottomlands of the Gros Ventre (hotspots 7-11), along Spring Gulch Road (hotspots 46), and near the intersection of Wyoming 22 and Teton Village Road (hotspots 44 and 45). Foxes are also occasionally seen on the northern section of Moose-Wilson Road (hotspot 41-42), areas of the Gros Ventre (hotspots 7-13), Snake River Overlook (hotspot 18), and Colter Bay area (hotspot 32).

Suggested April Itinerary: Before first light, head north from the town square to either the Gros Ventre area for beautiful first-light images of elk and bison on the ridges near the first overlook (hotspot 7) or near the town of Kelly and Teton Valley Ranch (hotspots 9-10). Many of the access roads to prime landscape locations will still be closed for winter but it is a relatively short walk to Mormon Row (hotspot 15) or down to the ponds of Schwabacher Landing (hotspot 17). Alternately, Snake River Overlook (hotspot 18) or Oxbow Bend (hotspot 27) areas are kept plowed and are excellent locations for first-light images of the Tetons. Next, travel north to the area of Pacific Creek to Colter Bay (hotspots 25, 27, 29, and 30-32) in search of bears. A drive east from Moran toward Togwotee Pass (hotspot 22) is also worth the trip, as occasional bears are near the highway feeding on dandelions. As you head back toward town, turn into Moose Junction and travel down Moose-Wilson Road (hotspots 41-43) to look for foxes, mule deer, and moose. You might also get lucky to see otters in the roadside ponds (hotspot 42).

After lunch at Dornan's or on the town square, head north again with a swing through the Moose-Wilson area (hotspots 41-42) followed by a repeat run up to Pacific Creek to Colter Bay area (hotspots 25, 27, 29, 30, 30-32) for bears. Wolves are very elusive but watch as you pass the National Elk Refuge, near the National Museum of Wildlife Art and Fish Hatchery (hotspots 4-6), for members of the Pinnacle Wolf Pack. They have a den site on the refuge property. Near sunset, travel back to one of the prime landscape locations or return to the Gros Ventre (hotspots 7-11). Elk bathed in late evening light is among the most beautiful sights to record.

May: Snow continues to melt during the month of May and the foliage almost explodes with the coming of spring. This is a time of abundant wildlife because they have survived the winter on dormant grasses and deciduous twigs. Boar and sow bears without cubs will be concentrated in the northern sections of the park and the section of highway between Moran and Togwotee Pass (see

April itinerary). Near the second to third week of May, sow bears with cubs will emerge from hibernation. They will be in the same locations as the other bears. Bears generally are active from dawn to dusk. They will forage for a few hours and then bed down for a few hours. Sows with cubs will also spend time nursing cubs.

Bison and elk will continue to be found in the Gros Ventre area (hotspots 7-13) and along the roadside between the elk refuge and Elk Flats (hotspots 5 and 21). Uinta ground squirrels also come out from hibernation near the first of the month. Ground squirrels are common along Mormon Row, Wolf Ranch Road, and Pacific Creek Road (hotspots 15, 19, and 25). Toward the end of the month, marmots can be seen along Pacific Creek Road and the Snake River Canyon area (hotspots 25 and 50).

Moose begin to come out of the bottomlands and are feeding on the aspens and willows as the leaves begin to appear on the trees. They will be visible along the northern section of Moose-Wilson Road, Teton Village Road, near Fish Creek in Wilson, the Gros Ventre, and along Pacific Creek Road (hotspots 41-42, 45, 7-13 and 25).

Toward the end of the month, badgers are seen along Wolf Ranch Road near the two ranch houses (hotspot 19) and foxes are still found in the Gros Ventre, Snake River Overlook, and Colter Bay areas (hotspot 9-13, 18, and 32). Osprey and eagles are relatively common along the northern section of Spring Gulch Road. Osprey are also common along the western end of Buffalo Valley Road (hotspot 24). Songbirds, such as the robins and mountain bluebirds, become more common, especially near the Murie Ranch and in the Mormon Row area (hotspots 41 and 15).

Suggested May Itinerary: Most of the access roads to prime landscape locations will still be snowed in during the first two weeks of May but will open toward the latter half of May. Toward the end of May, the closed section of Teton Park Road will reopen (hotspots 35-39). Snake River Overlook and Oxbow Bend are open year-around (hotspots 18 and 27). Similar to the April itinerary, before first light, head north from the town square to either the Gros Ventre area for beautiful sunrise images of elk and bison on the ridges near the first overlook or near the town of Kelly and Teton Valley Ranch (hotspots 7 and 11). Or head north and watch for elk and bison along the highway that are gradually migrating from their lowland winter range back to the northern areas of the park.

Next, head north to the area of Pacific Creek to Colter Bay in search of bears (hotspots 25, 27, 29, 30-32). Also, a drive east from Moran toward Togwotee Pass (hotspot 22) is also worth the trip as occasional bears are near the highway feeding on dandelions. Boars and sows without cubs (bears) will be feeding near the roads the first two weeks of the month. Sows with cubs will start appearing the latter half of the month. As you head back toward town, turn down Wolf Ranch Road (if open) and watch for badgers (hotspot 19). Badgers are nocturnal, but they have babies to feed in the spring, so they are more active during the daytime. Then continue south to Moose Junction and travel down Moose-Wilson Road looking for foxes, mule deer, and moose (hotspots 41-43).

After lunch at Dornan's or on the town square, head north again with a swing through the Moose-Wilson area and Wolf Ranch Road for badgers (hotspots 41-43 and 19). Follow this with a repeat run-up to the Pacific Creek to Colter Bay area for bears (hotspots 25, 27, 29, and 30-32). Near sunset, travel back to one of the prime landscape locations or return south of the Elk Ranch area in search of elk near the highway or the Gros Ventre area (hotspots 21, and 7-14).

May is also the start of wildflower season with the arrowleaf balsamroot among the first to flower. The balsamroot is followed by similar yellow flowers of the Mule's-Ear. Many other wildflowers, such as lupine, bloom in May and early June. Antelope flats east of Mormon Row, Cattleman's Landing, and Lupine Meadows are ideal locations for landscape images that include the wildflowers and the iconic Tetons (hotspots 14-15, 28 and 38). Generally, it is best to wait an hour or so after first light when the soft morning light hits the wildflowers and the Tetons simultaneously.

June-July: June and July are the hot months in the Tetons. Of course, if you are from the south, temperatures in the low to mid-80s will seem like a comfortable spring or autumn day. However, animals have a heavy coat of hair and many will bed down for the midday to avoid the heat. Bears will typically head into the mountains during these months. Early mornings and late afternoons are the best times to view wildlife during these months. The wildflowers that blanket the open areas of Antelope Flats, Cattleman's Landing, and Lupine Meadows will quickly fade as the heat rises (hotspots 14-15, 28, and 38).

During the first couple weeks of June, elk will still be migrating from the refuge area northward. They will be feeding on grasses in the Gros Ventre and along the highway (hotspots 5 and 21). Toward the latter part of June and all of July, elk will be more difficult to find as they avoid the heat and stay under the tree canopy. During these periods, the area near Lupine Meadows is a prime spot to find them (hotspots 38-39). Pregnant elk cows congregate in the Willow Flats area during the month of June to give birth under the cover of the thick willows (hotspot 29). Also, watch this area for wolves, coyotes, and bears; these predators are drawn to the area by the newborns.

Moose will become more prevalent as they inhabit the bottomlands of the Gros Ventre near the river (hotspots 7-9). Watch for moose near the overlooks. Moose are also seen at Blacktail Ponds, Schwabacher Landing, along Moose-Wilson Road, and from Teton Village to Wyoming 22 (hotspots 17 and 44). Like elk, moose will be most active in the mornings and evenings, remaining under deep cover in the midday. Moose calves are born the first two weeks of May. Moose are generally solitary animals (not herding animals like elk and bison), so you will generally see a single bull or a cow-calf pair. It is not unusual for the cow moose to give birth to twins.

Bison are moving or have moved to their summer range near Elk Ranch (hotspot 21). Pronghorn have also returned from their winter range and are visible in the Elk Ranch area. Bison move about and will be found in herds between Elk Ranch to Kelly on the Gros Ventre (hotspots 21, 20, 19, and 9-15).

Grizzly and black bears will still be feeding on dandelions during the first couple weeks of June. As the season progresses, grizzlies will head up into the mountains to avoid the summer heat. However, many times sows with cubs will remain down in the valley, particularly near the heavy tree canopy of Colter Bay and Dump Road (hotspots 31-32). Black bears are typically spotted from Pacific Creek area to Colter Bay and on Teton Park Road from the dam south past the Signal Mountain area (hotspots 25-32 and 34-36).

Badgers will still be active during the daytime during the month of June but will be very difficult to observe in July, as they are nocturnal. When badger babies are young, they require near twenty-four hour care by the parents, giving us the opportunity to see them during the daylight. Beavers will also become more active in June and July. They are most active at first light or the hour before sunset, particularly in the ponds at Schwabacher Landing and the ponds along Moose-Wilson Road (hotspots 17 and 42-43).

Suggested June-July Itinerary: By the first week of June, all roads are open and the south entrance to Yellowstone is also open (hotspot 33). Tourist season is in full swing with lots of traffic and buses. However, there are still abundant opportunities to view and photograph wildlife and landscapes.

A suggested itinerary would be to arrive at the barns of Mormon Row before first light (hotspot 15). As the sun begins to rise, alpenglow illuminates the Tetons with soft glowing illumination. This fades quickly and as the sun clears the mountains to the east. The barns and the Tetons will be bathed in a beautiful golden light that is perfect for photography. Schwabacher Landing, Snake River Overlook, and Oxbow Bend are also prime locations for images at first light (hotspots 17-18 and 27). After sunrise, check the Gros Ventre overlook area for moose that will be feeding on willows and cottonwoods by the river (hotspots 7-9). Check Moose-Wilson Road and Blacktail Ponds for moose near the ponds (hotspots 41-43 and 16). Then head up to the Pacific Creek to Colter Bay area for bears (hotspots 25-32). June and July are particularly excellent times to photograph the marmots with their babies along Pilgrim Creek Road (hotspot 30). Return to Elk Flats for bison and pronghorn. Also watch for coyotes, as they tend to hunt frequently in the Elk Flats region (hotspot 21).

After lunch, Elk Flats is an excellent location for viewing wildlife in the middle of the day (hotspot 21). Bison will have their "red dog" calves and pronghorn will have their babies in the open grassland areas. Also look along Wolf Ranch Road in June for badgers, though they will be rarely sighted in July as they are nocturnal and the badger babies do not need as much care as when younger. Uinta ground squirrels are common along Wolf Ranch Road and are particularly photogenic with their young (hotspot 19). In the late afternoon, drive north again to look for bears with cubs or head south to Moose-Wilson Road, Schwabacher Landing, or the Gros Ventre area to look for moose (hotspots 41-43, 17, and 7-13). Alternately, drive the inner loop Teton Park Road looking for black bears near the Signal Mountain area and elk near Lupine Meadows (hotspots 34-39).

Sunsets over the Tetons are generally not as spectacular as other places because the pollution level is so low. Nevertheless, Jenny Lake, Oxbow Bend, Blacktail Pond, and Snake River Overlook are prime locations for sunset images (hotspots 36, 27, 16, and 18). A rarely visited location is Curtis Canyon; try a wide panoramic shot of the entire Teton Range from this location (hotspot 2).

August: August is the last of the high summer temperatures and the animals will continue to be most prevalent soon after the dawn and prior to dusk. Much of information given above for June-July also applies to August. The one notable exception is for black bears. Moose-Wilson Road, from LSR to the overlook, is bordered by shrubs with berries (hotspots 41-43). These shrubs include hawthorn, chokecherry, and huckleberry; these berries ripen in August and black bears come out to consume the berries. Traffic along this road will be heavy as this is the height of tourist season but the bears do not seem to mind. They are intent on obtaining berries to fatten up for the long winter ahead. Typically, the bears will be feeding on the berries near the roadside. Bears can be found on the ground and in the shrubs. Toward the end of August, the Uinta ground squirrels enter their burrows for their long winter hibernation.

Suggested August Itinerary: The itinerary of June-July applies equally well for August. However, spending more time along Moose-Wilson Road will provide an opportunity for seeing and photographing a plethora of black bears (hotspots 41-43). Parking is near non-existent along this stretch of road and it is illegal to stop in this area. The volunteer ranger brigade members will be watchful. The volunteer rangers are charged with helping protect the bears and tourists. Although they are volunteers, they do have the authority of the park service. Failure to follow their directives will incur a quick visit by a park ranger with full abilities to enforce park regulations.

September-October: The elk and moose rut begins near the middle of September and extends into the first week or so of October. Bull elk will be gathering their harems in preparation for the reproduction period. Bull moose will also be trying to attract suitable mates.

Early morning and late afternoon is the best time to observe the elk rut. Teton Park Road, between Windy Point and Lupine Meadows, will be alive with elk activity (hotspot 37-39). Frequently, the bulls are bugling as a warning to other bulls to stay clear and as an attractant for available cows. As a herding animal, bull elk can attract five or more cows during the rut. On occasion, there will be fights between bulls.

The Gros Ventre area is the best place to photograph and observe the moose rut. The area near the Gros Ventre campground and within the campground is prime rut habitat (hotspot 8). Fish Creek in Wilson is another prime area to observe and photograph the moose rut (hotspot 45). The bulls and cows are especially photogenic during this period as they are in prime condition and the cottonwood and aspen trees have begun to change as autumn approaches.

As summer temperatures abate, you can feel the coming winter. The bears can, too. Grizzly bears return from the upland areas to the lowland meadows to forage. Nearly any time of the day, bears can be found near the Pilgrim Creek area and north to Colter Bay (hotspots 30-32). Bears will be digging in the meadows for biscuitroot and other food items. It is during this time that the marmots retire for their winter hibernation.

Toward the latter part of October, elk and bison begin their autumn migration toward the National Elk Refuge (hotspot 5). Watch for these large animals near the roadside and in the roadside meadows; they will also begin feeding in the meadows of the Gros Ventre (hotspots 7-13). When driving, be especially careful after dark as these animals have dark coats and are difficult to see.

The moose rut also ends after the first week of October and moose begin feeding on bitterbrush in the open meadows between Kelly and Ditch Creek (hotspots 9-13). As many as thirty moose can be sighted on a single day foraging in these areas. Occasionally, bulls will have some residual testosterone and will do some sparing.

With the approach of autumn, landscape images in the Oxbow Bend area are especially beautiful (hotspot 27). The cottonwood and aspen trees will be yellow with color against the gray mountains that are capped with white snow. Both early morning and late afternoon provide opportunities for wonderful images, especially when the wind is calm, and the Oxbow lake water surface is glassy.

Suggested September-October Itinerary: Tourist season is beginning to wind down, but wildlife season is heating up. Mornings are an excellent time to spend in the Gros Ventre area for the moose rut followed by a trip north for bears near the Pilgrim Creek area (hotspots 7-13 and 30). It is good to pack drinks and food, as activity can be so fierce that you may not make it back to town until well after dark. In the late afternoon, head down the inner loop road (Teton Park Road) to observe and photograph elk in the rut (hotspots 34-40). Photographing moose, elk, and bears can easily fill an entire day. Plan for landscape images at first light followed by wildlife images for the balance of the day.

November-December: Typically, it will snow in earnest in November and start to accumulate significantly in December. Elk and bison continue to migrate in early November and generally most reach the winter grounds by mid to late-November. Occasionally, a couple bison will not migrate and most will succumb to starvation if they remain in the Elk Flats area (hotspot 21). Moose continue to forage in the meadows of the Gros Ventre during the month of November and the first half of December (hotspots 7-13). Moose lose their antlers starting near the end of November and continuing into late December. As deep snow covers the sagebrush meadows in the latter part of December, moose will move to the lowland areas near the river.

Toward the latter part of October, bighorn sheep begin migrating from the uplands to Miller Butte on the elk refuge (hotspot 1). First, the yews and lambs arrive but are soon followed by the rams toward the middle of November. The bighorn sheep rut is generally the first part of December. This is a time of intense activity between the rams. The crack of horns of two opposing rams can be heard from a significant distance. All this activity occurs very near the roadside, typically a couple hours after first light through late afternoon (hotspot 1).

Like the bighorn sheep, mountain goats also move to lower elevations as the snow accumulates. This provides an ideal opportunity to view and photograph them as they are near the highway along the Snake River Canyon (hotspot 50).

Suggested November-December Itinerary: Before first light, take the opportunity for some landscape images of the iconic Tetons or the Mormon barns (hotspot 15). Follow that with a tour through the Gros Ventre area for the abundant moose that will be feeding in the meadows between Kelly and Ditch Creek (hotspots 9-10). A drive up to Moose Junction and down Moose-Wilson Road is worthwhile as this is the time of year that mule deer are preparing for the rut and foxes are on the hunt for the next meal (hotspots 41-43).

Between midday and mid-afternoon, activity near Miller Butte will be at its highest (hotspot 1). A person could spend most of the day just watching the bighorn sheep rams as they vie for rights of the yews. The best part is the proximity: the sheep are down by the roadside during these "fights." Remain in your vehicle with your arms inside the cabin. In fact, at times the sheep will attempt to lick salt from your vehicle. The Elk Refuge and U.S. Fish and Wildlife Service requests that you do not stop long enough for this to happen.

Elk generally are on the west side of Miller's Butte but occasionally they are near the south entrance of the refuge (hotspot 1). During November and December, most bulls still have their full complement of antlers, as these are not shed until after the first of the year.

Use of this guide

The fifty hotspots are scattered around the park and the local Jackson Hole area. The directions start from the town square of Jackson. Each hotspot includes directions from the town square and is in order of appearance. However, it is also possible to enter the park from the southwest (Teton Village), east (Dubois area), or the north. Just start your journey in the book at the hotspot that most closely matches your entrance point.

During tourist season, seldom will you be the first to see any animal. However, anytime you are driving, and you see an ample collection of cars parked on the side of the road, it is best to park and walk to the area of people. Typically, there will be a park ranger helping to keep visitors safe but, at other times, you might need to rely on your own sense of safety. Always remember that animals in the Tetons are wild and powerful. Like people, they are relatively predictable. However, on occasion, animals will act in unpredictable ways. It is best to assume they also have bad days, are not feeling like tolerating humans that day, etc.

Each hotspot has animals that frequent that area. There are also camera recommendations for those with advanced or professional equipment. Do not feel that these recommendations leave you behind if you have a point-and-shoot or a camera phone. There are accessories that attach to camera phones and many point-and-shoot cameras rival the quality of professional cameras just ten years ago. By following the recommendations of this guide, you will return home with some breathtaking images to share with your family and friends.

The Tetons are among the most amazing locations on our planet. Use whatever camera you own to document your trip. Seldom does anyone return home without a few images that get enlarged and hung in their office or their home. Most visitors are on vacation, so it's tempting to sleep in and relax. Instead, wake up early and relax in the midday. Few places on Earth are more beautiful than the Tetons at first light. Animals are also more attractive with the soft golden glow of early morning and the golden glow of the late afternoon light.

MY FIELD NOTES:

Map #1

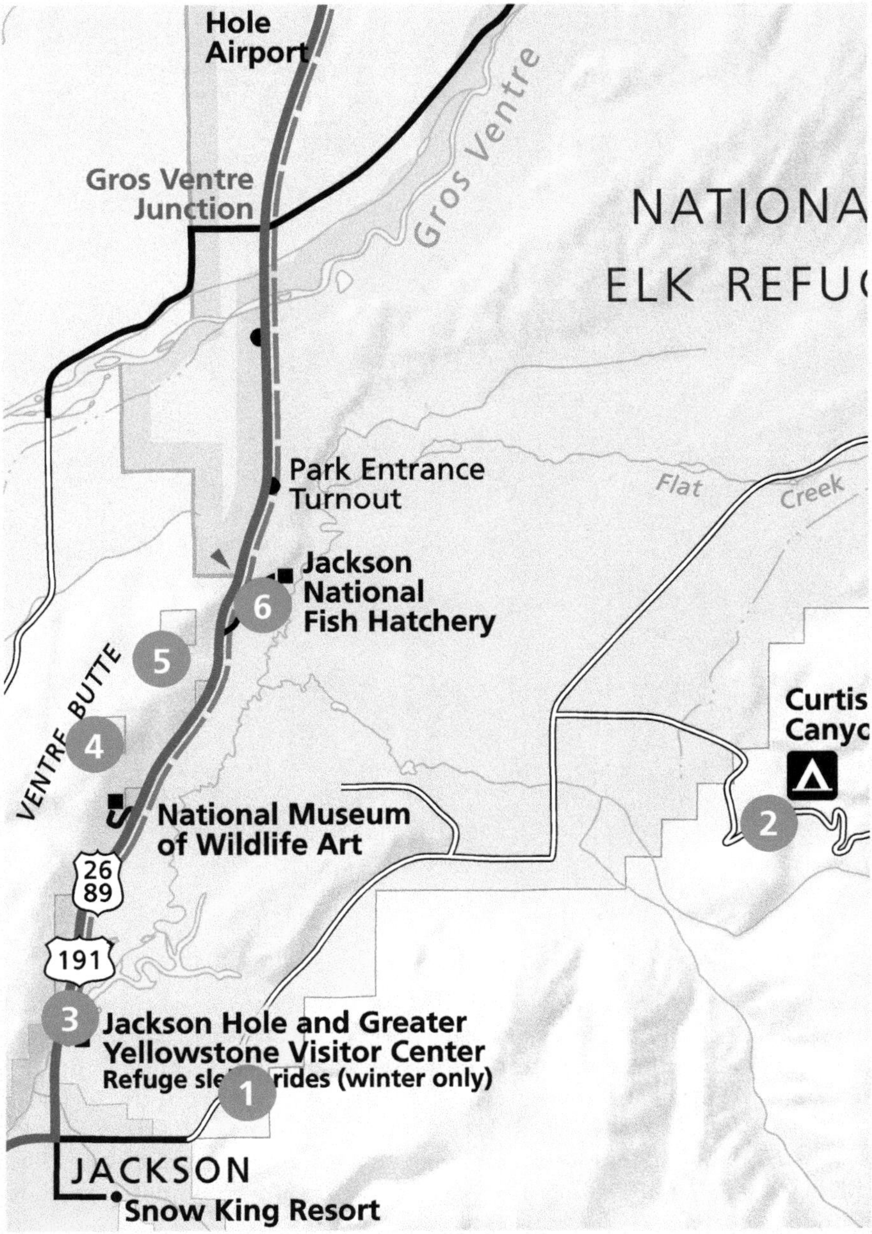

Hole
Airport
Gros Ventre
Junction
Gros Ventre
NATIONA
ELK REFU
Park Entrance
Turnout
Flat
Creek
Jackson
National
Fish Hatchery
6
5
BUTTE
VENTRE
4
Curtis
Canyo
2
National Museum
of Wildlife Art
26
89
191
3
Jackson Hole and Greater
Yellowstone Visitor Center
Refuge sle rides (winter only)
1
JACKSON
Snow King Resort

HOTSPOT #1

MAP 1

National Elk Refuge
(South Entrance)

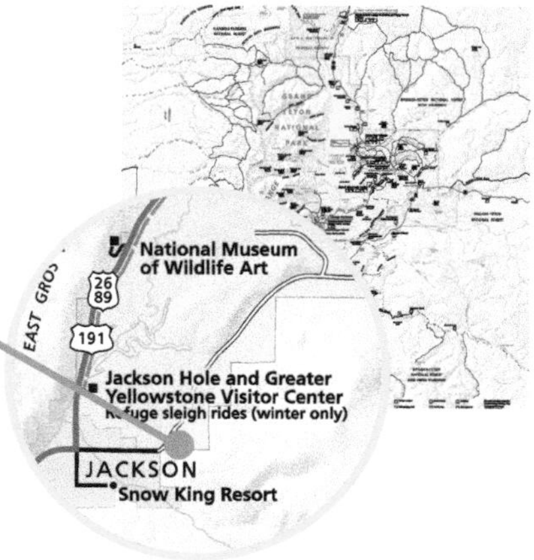

HIGHLIGHTS:

In winter, elk are frequently near the south entrance gate, occasionally to the east of Miller's Butte, and in the meadow north of Miller's Butte. As snow depth accumulates, bighorn sheep descend the mountains to overwinter in the refuge from mid-November until late April. Occasionally, pronghorn are seen near the butte. Bison also overwinter in the refuge but they are fed in the northern part of the refuge so they are seldom seen near the access roads in winter. The primary wildlife in the refuge from late spring to early autumn is numerous ground squirrels.

DIRECTIONS

Mileage from Jackson Town Square

From Jackson town square travel east on Broadway for 1.0 mile until the road ends then turn left into the refuge. Miller's Butte is west of the roadside after you pass the Miller House and the ponds. At Twin Creek Ranch (4.6 miles), the road makes a sharp left turn; the road is closed past this point in winter to protect wildlife.

WILDLIFE IN AREA:

Bighorn Sheep:

Bighorn sheep descend the high country to overwinter in the refuge in late October and return to the high country in early May. In early mornings and late evenings, they can be seen on the upper ridges of Miller's Butte. During the day they are frequently near the road. The bighorn rut is approximately the second week of December; this is an exciting time for watching and photographing the rams. Rams head butt with tremendous force as they compete for breeding rights with the ewes.

Elk:

Elk frequent the refuge during the heavy snow periods (roughly November through April). During the 2016–2017 winter, refuge staff estimated elk numbers at approximately 8,500. They usually congregate on the west side of Miller's Butte but can occasionally be seen in the meadows to the east, north and south of Miller's Butte.

Predators:

During the winter, elk, and pronghorn carcasses are relatively frequent. Golden and bald eagles, coyotes, foxes, and wolves visit the carcasses. Wolves generally visit late evening to early morning. However, wolves can be seen in the distant meadows during the day. Infrequently, there are weasels (ermine) between the south entrance and the first parking turnout. During the non-winter months, badgers, coyotes, and raptors are plentiful as they feed on ground squirrels.

Ground Squirrels:

Uinta ground squirrels are plentiful along the roadway leading into the refuge. They emerge from their burrows in April and return to hibernation in August or September.

Site Specific Photography Tips

Elk: Lenses in the 100 to 600mm range are best for photographing elk at the refuge, depending on how much background you wish to include.

Bighorn Sheep: During the daytime, most any lens will work great for the bighorns as they are near the road, at times on the road licking salt from cars. Images from the butte ridges are best with lenses in the 400 to 600mm range. Rut activity will generally be best photographed with a 200 to 400mm lens and a higher shutter speed to stop action.

Ground Squirrel: Ground squirrels can be a bit skittish at first. Choose a location with a rich concentration of squirrels, remain still and the squirrels will soon resume normal activities. Use a 300 to 600mm lens, focus on the nearest eye and use an aperture of f5.6 to f8 to blur part of the background.

Predators: When animals die, the carcasses attract predators. Lenses in the 300 to 600mm range are best for predators as they can be shy. Wolves are most active at dawn and dusk whereas coyotes are more active in the daytime. Eagles will frequently flee when you set up your equipment but many times will return quickly to the carcass to resume feeding. Excellent flight shots are possible as the eagles circle and land near the carcass.

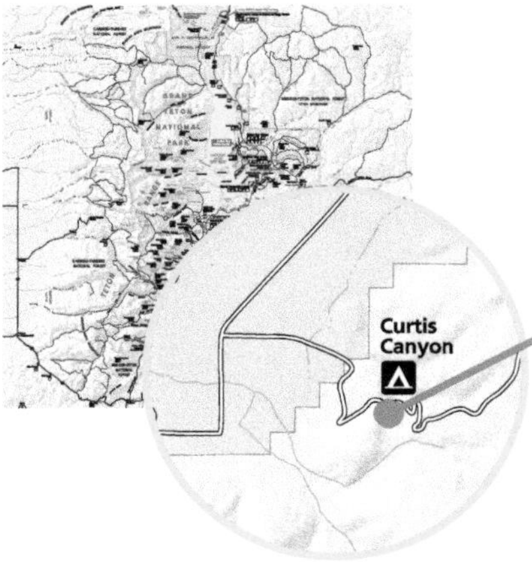

HOTSPOT #2

Twin Creek Ranch to Curtis Canyon

HIGHLIGHTS:

The Curtis Canyon viewpoint is a premier spot to obtain a panoramic shot of the Teton Mountain range. The drive from Twin Creek to Curtis Canyon passes through sagebrush meadows; elk, pronghorn, eagles, and coyotes are common in the area during late fall to early spring. The road from Twin Creek to Curtis Canyon is closed after snow accumulates. It typically opens in the spring after the snow melts and the roadbed dries out sufficiently for vehicle traffic (roughly mid-May).

DIRECTIONS

Mileage from Jackson Town Square

From Jackson town square travel east on Broadway for 1.0 mile, turn left into the refuge. Travel 4.6 miles and turn left, follow this road for 1.1 miles and turn right at the Curtis Canyon sign. Continue into the Bridger-Teton National Forest to the Curtis Canyon viewpoint.

MAP 1

WILDLIFE IN AREA:

Coyotes, foxes, elk, and pronghorn are possible from the refuge entrance to the viewpoint. Arriving prior to sunrise will provide one of the best panoramic views of the Teton mountain range, a view seldom recorded by others that visit the park.

Site Specific Photography Tips

Landscapes: Wide-angle lenses are best for capturing the vast expanse of the Tetons. In fact, a multi-stitch panorama would make a wide wall-hanging print. Curtis Canyon is to the east of the Tetons so the morning sun will highlight the Tetons as it rises early. Early mornings provide stunning views of alpenglow on the mountains; a bit later in the morning would be best for capturing well-illuminated wildflowers with the mountains. At times, Jackson Hole has nice sunsets. A unique option would be astrophotography of the Tetons.

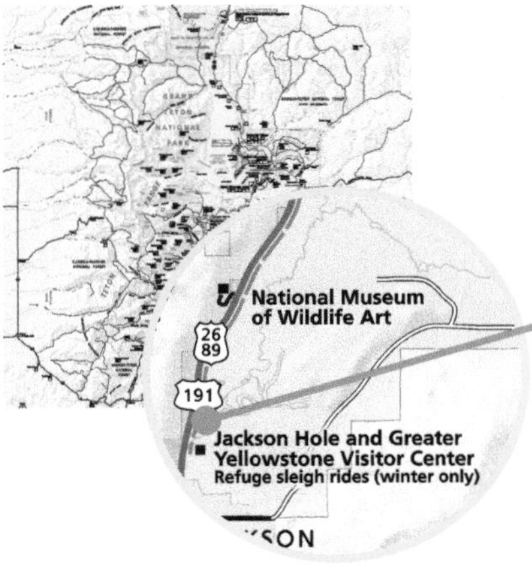

HOTSPOT #3

Flat Creek at Visitor's Center

MAP 1

HIGHLIGHTS:

The pond attracts a variety of birds including Trumpeter Swans, American Coots, ducks, Great Blue Herons, and Canada geese.

DIRECTIONS

Mileage from Jackson Town Square

From Jackson town square, travel north on Highway 89 for 0.5 miles. Turn right into the parking area of the visitor's center.

MAP 1

WILDLIFE IN AREA:

Trumpeter Swans:

Trumpeter Swans, North America's largest native waterfowl, with a wingspan of six feet, are impressive birds. They are the heaviest flying birds (twenty-six pounds) needing a one hundred yard open water "runway" for takeoff. Swans frequently fly to the Flat Creek pond from the Swan Pond (#48) south of the city center. Swans and other waterfowl are in this area from early spring through mid-autumn.

Site Specific Photography Tips

Swans: Because of the size of swans, excellent flight images are possible with little experience. Lenses in the 100 to 600mm range are best for flight images. Nice images of swans floating on the water are also possible.

Other Waterfowl: The fence is relatively low in some areas making better images possible. Occasionally, a Great Blue Heron will perch on the fence posts.

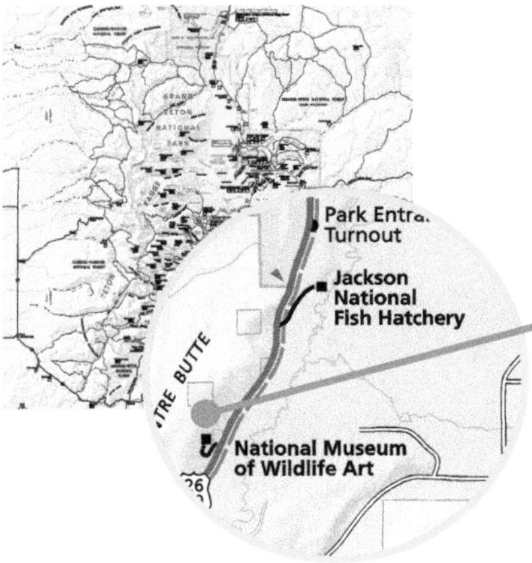

HOTSPOT #4

MAP 1

National Museum of Wildlife Art

HIGHLIGHTS:

During winter, mule deer feed on the west slopes of the hillside. Using a spotting scope from the museum parking area, wolves can occasionally be seen in the National Elk Refuge to the east. Elk are abundant in the refuge from approximately November through April. Marmots live in the rock crevices near the driveway to the museum. They come out of hibernation in April and return to hibernation in August.

DIRECTIONS

Mileage from Jackson Town Square

From Jackson town square, travel north on Highway 89 for 2.9 miles. Turn left onto museum drive and wind up the driveway. Parking is available to the south or beyond the museum to the north.

WILDLIFE IN AREA:

Wolves:

Wolves can occasionally be seen from the museum overlook using a spotting scope, binoculars or a long telephoto lens. Wolves tend to bed down during the day so it is best to look for them early in the morning or late in the day. However, the wolves will be distant, approximately ¼ to ½ mile, so images from this location will be little more than a record of the sighting.

Marmots:

The marmots are in the rock crevices and the grass areas along the driveway to the museum from late spring to early autumn. They tend to be most active in the sunshine. These marmots tend to be a bit skittish; the marmots on Pilgrim Creek Road (#30) or at the golf course on Spring Gulch Road (#46) are more tolerant of people.

Site Specific Photography Tips

Mule Deer: Mule deer are relatively tolerant of vehicles. Using a beanbag, good images can be obtained from your car window. Deer are herding animals; one deer will watch for predators as the others forage. However, as a loud truck passes or other significant noise, most deer will pick-up their heads from the ground, resulting in a good image.

Marmot: These marmots are a bit skittish; patience is a real virtue with these marmots, as they will hide in the crevices for a long time before coming out to investigate.

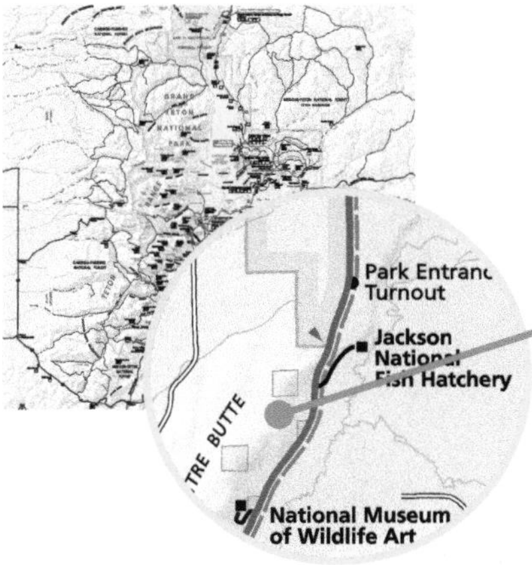

HOTSPOT #5

National Elk Refuge, west side

MAP 1

HIGHLIGHTS:

As the snow begins to accumulate, elk and bison begin their migration to the National Elk Refuge. Between 5-9,000 elk overwinter at the refuge. Elk enter the refuge from the undeveloped area to the east and north or they can enter through the elevated elk jumps through the fence on the west boundary. In October and November, elk walk along the fence line until they reach the elk jumps, then jump down from the elevated hill into the refuge. In early spring, elk and bison exit the refuge at the north end near the Gros Ventre River.

DIRECTIONS

Mileage from Jackson Town Square

From Jackson town square, travel north on Highway 89 for 0.6 miles. The elk refuge fencing extends north to Gros Ventre Junction (6.9 miles). Use one of the pullouts along Highway 89 to view animals within the refuge and on the hills to the west of the highway.

MAP 1

WILDLIFE IN AREA:

Elk:

Elk congregate on the west side of Miller's Butte (the hillside in the refuge seen from the area of the National Museum of Wildlife Art). Thousands of elk herd together in this area. At times, they are close enough for nice images but most times, they are a beautiful binocular or spotting scope sight.

Wolves:

Wolves can occasionally be seen from the turnouts along Highway 89 using a spotting scope, binoculars, or a long telephoto lens.

Bison:

During winter, bison are fed in the north area of the refuge and are seldom seen. However, during fall and spring migration, bison are near the roadside as they move from the Elk Ranch area to the refuge.

Winter Sleigh Rides:

Horse-pulled sleigh rides are an excellent way to safely get close to the elk and learn a bit about the history of the refuge. The rides are fun, romantic, and entertaining but they are in an open sleigh so dress for warmth. Take along your camera with a moderate telephoto lens. The sleigh driver will get relatively close to the elk. Tickets and shuttles for the one-hour sleigh ride are available at the visitor's center.

Site Specific Photography Tips

Elk Photography Tips: A 500 to 600mm lens is best for photographing the elk at the refuge but a 100 to 400mm is sufficient during the sleigh ride. During migration, late fall, and early spring, elk are frequently along the roadside. Be careful when driving, especially at night, as the elk are frequently on the road.

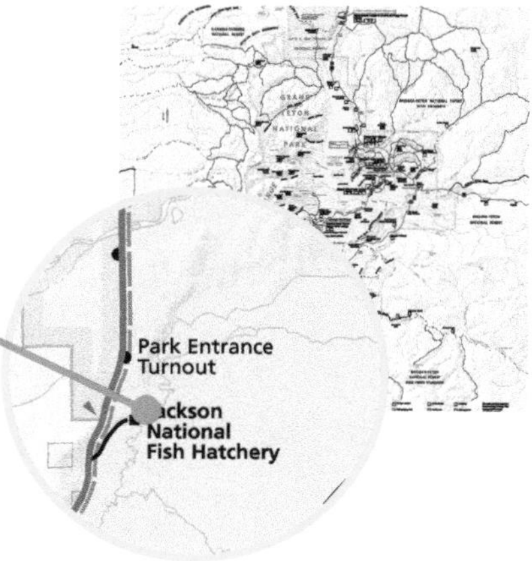

HOTSPOT #6

Fish Hatchery

HIGHLIGHTS:

At this location, winter is the best time to see mammals. However, spring through autumn is best for water birds. Wolves, mule deer, and elk can occasionally be seen from the intersection of Highway 89 and Fish Hatchery Road. Scope into the refuge to the east for wolves and elk. Look to the west across Highway 89, on the hillside, for mule deer. Numerous duck species including bufflehead, goldeneyes, and mallards are present in the fish hatchery pond (4.4 miles).

DIRECTIONS

Mileage from Jackson Town Square

Travel north on Highway 89 for 3.9 miles. After you pass the visitor's center on the right, turn right onto Fish Hatchery Road and travel an additional 0.4 miles to the parking areas.

WILDLIFE IN AREA:

Wolves:

Wolves of the Pinnacle Pack are occasionally observed in the National Elk Refuge from the intersection of Highway 89 and Fish Hatchery Road. They are easier to spot once snow falls.

Water birds:

In mid-autumn, Trumpeter swans visit the pond until it freezes over. American coots and ducks, such as mallards and goldeneyes, are frequently feeding in the pond. Canada geese are the most common bird in the area.

Mule Deer:

Mule deer forage along the roadside and on the hillside west of Highway 89. They are most frequent in wintertime.

Site Specific Photography Tips

Wolves: Wolves are one of the most iconic animals of the park. Seeing a wolf, even from a distance, is emotional. Seldom are wolves closing enough for a frame-filling image. However, distant "record" images are possible with a 400 to 600mm lens or using spotting scopes.

Water birds: The pond surface is a couple feet below the fence area, so good images of birds on the water surface are obtained by getting low to the ground and shooting through the fencing. Because birds typically fly into the wind to take off and land, images of birds landing or taking off are best with a north or south wind at this location.

Map #2

COVERING HOTSPOTS #7-17

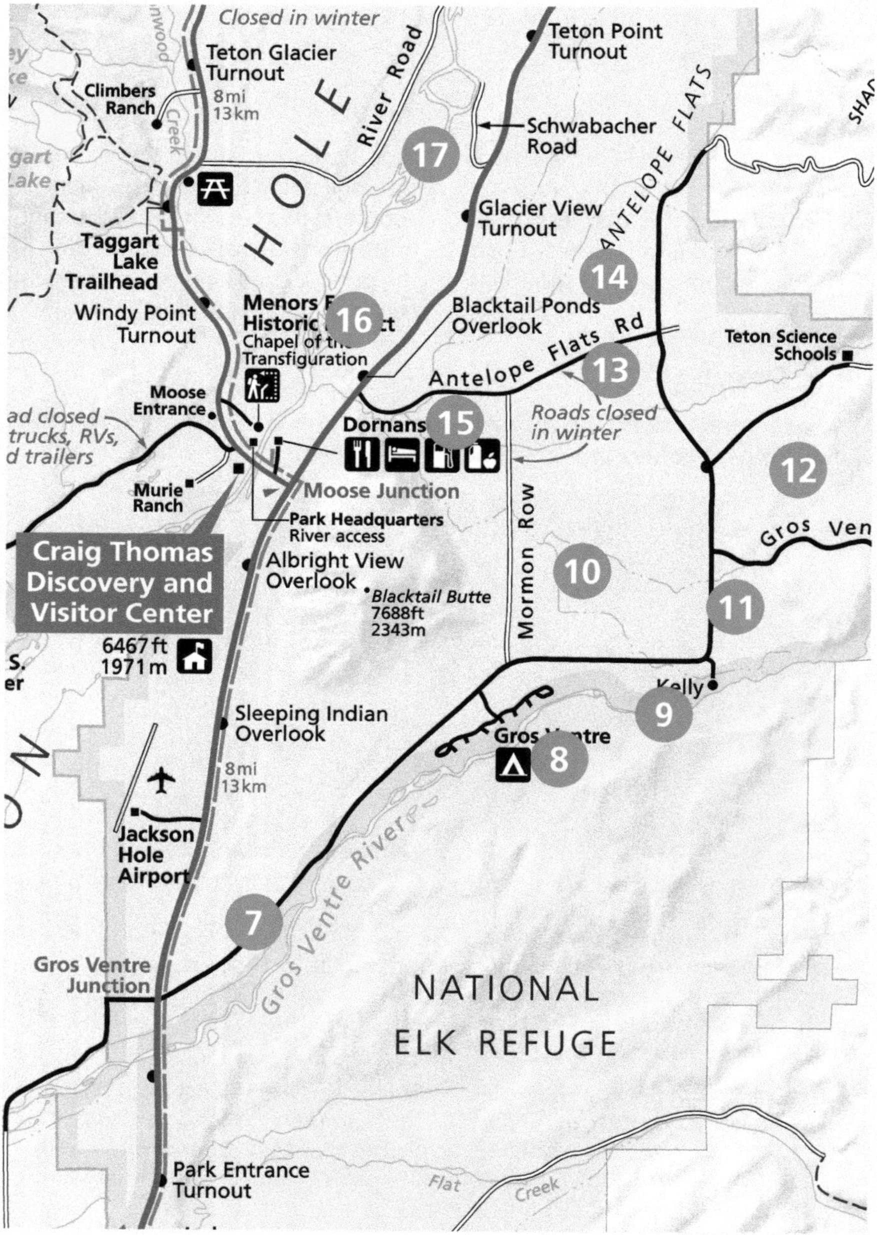

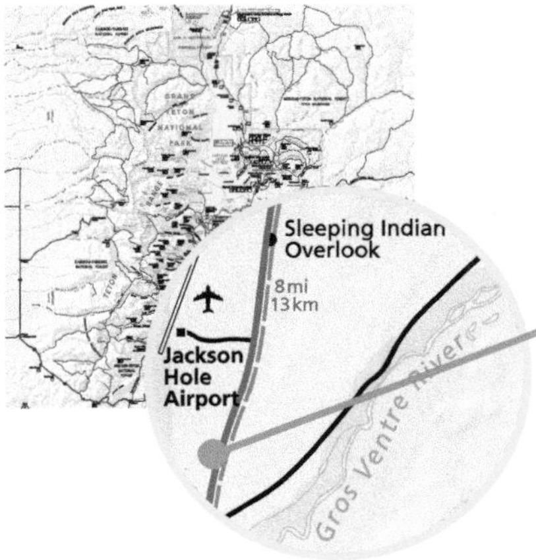

HOTSPOT #7

Gros Ventre Overlook

HIGHLIGHTS:

The Gros Ventre area (hotspots 7-13) is the most underrated area of the park. Moose, elk, bison, ground squirrels, foxes, coyotes, and wolves can be found in this area. Moose are frequent visitors to the overlook area that includes the Gros Ventre River. Bison and elk are frequently found on the ridgeline to the north. Moose, elk, coyotes, and bison use the meadows between the overlook and the ridgeline.

DIRECTIONS

Mileage from Jackson Town Square

Travel north on Highway 89 to Gros Ventre Junction (6.9 miles). Turn right on Gros Ventre Road and continue past the first two turnouts (8.1 and 9.0 miles) to the overlook (9.4 miles). The ridgeline is the berm to the north of the road.

WILDLIFE IN AREA:

MAP 2

Moose:

Moose, the largest member of the deer family, are frequently found along the Gros Ventre River area from late spring through early fall eating willow, aspen and cottonwood leaves. As snow begins to accumulate, moose move to the meadows to feed on bitterbrush. Once the bitterbrush is completely covered by deep snow, moose move to forest canopy areas and feed on deciduous twigs, Douglas fir, and subalpine fir.

Moose antlers fall off every year around the end of December. Park regulations state the antlers must not be collected or removed from the area. Antler regrowth begins in April; during the growing period, a thick skin covering known as velvet covers the bone. Prior to the rut (reproduction period), the velvet peels off and exposes the bone. This occurs near the beginning of September and the rut occurs near the end of September-beginning of October.

Bison and Elk:

Bison and elk move through the area during spring and fall migration. Both feed on grasses in the lowland areas and meadows, though they frequently are found on the ridgeline. Predators are easier to see from an elevated area, giving them a measure of protection.

Coyotes:

Coyotes are a frequent visitor to the meadows in winter as they hunt for rodents. They typically hunt the meadows below the ridgeline.

Site Specific Photography Tips

Moose: A 300 to 600mm lens is best for photographing the moose. Although moose seem very friendly, they can be dangerous, especially in the spring when the cows have their babies to protect and in the fall when the bulls are in the rut.

Bison and Elk: Lenses in the 100 to 400mm range work well for both bison and elk, especially when they are on the ridgeline. If you are lucky, you can get both the animal and the Tetons in the same shot. Use a small aperture (such as f16) so the animal and the mountains are both in focus.

Coyote: Coyotes tend to avoid the roadsides however when they cross from one side to the other, lenses in the 100 to 400mm range are sufficient. Shooting from the car window next to the roadside will yield better results as the coyotes seldom approach human figures.

HOTSPOT #8

Gros Ventre Campground

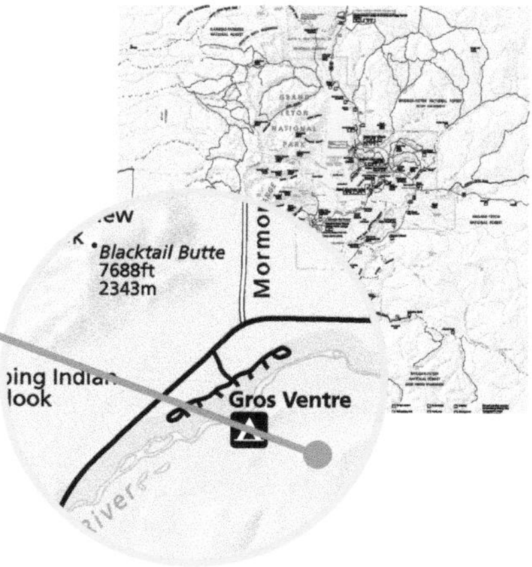

MAP 2

HIGHLIGHTS:

The campground and Gros Ventre River behind and the meadow in front is a prime location for moose. Because of the campers in the area, there are few other animals.

DIRECTIONS

Mileage from Jackson Town Square

Travel north on Highway 89 to Gros Ventre Junction (6.9 miles). Turn right on Gros Ventre Road; continue to campground entrance (11.6 miles), turn right and proceed into campground. The public is permitted in the campground but be respectful of occupied camping areas.

WILDLIFE IN AREA:

Moose:

Moose are frequently found in the campground area including the Gros Ventre River wetland area behind the campground and the meadow in front. At times, cow moose will birth their babies (first couple weeks in May) in the campground because wolves will generally not enter a place with a high density of humans. The rut is also an active time (late September and early October) for moose in the campground area.

Site Specific Photography Tips

Moose: A 300 to 600mm lens is best for photographing the moose. Be careful of moose in the campground area as cows with young calves are very protective. During the rut, bulls are aggressive and unpredictable. The cows are being chased by the bulls, so they are a bit unpredictable also. Caution is necessary for your own safety but also the safety of the moose.

Some of the best images are possible in the Gros Ventre River area behind the campground, especially during the rut. The cottonwood and willow leaves turn yellow providing a beautiful background. From sunrise until approximately 10 am, beautiful soft light blankets the river valley and illuminates the moose. In addition, there are no fire-pits, picnic tables, RV campers and tents to obstruct your images.

HOTSPOT **#9**

Town of Kelly

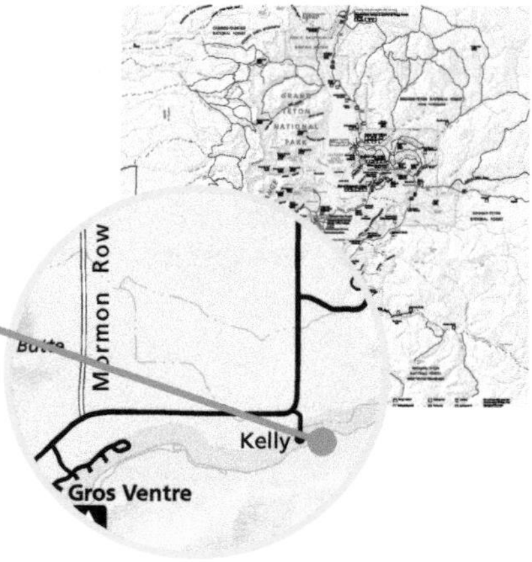

MAP 2

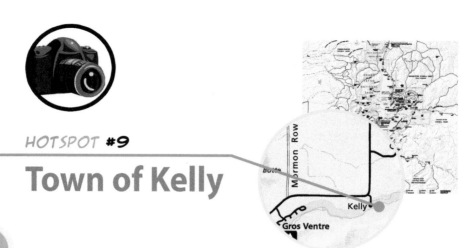

HIGHLIGHTS:

Kelly is a small town located on the Gros Ventre River consisting of houses ranging in size from tiny cabins to large homes. Kelly is an area with a healthy concentration of mule deer from autumn to early spring and bison from late spring to autumn.

DIRECTIONS

Mileage from Jackson Town Square

Travel north on Highway 89 to Gros Ventre Junction (6.9 miles). Turn right on Gros Ventre Road; continue to the town of Kelly (14.0 miles).

WILDLIFE IN AREA:

Mule Deer:

Mule deer use the residential area of Kelly for protection from wolves. The deer forage in the meadows around Kelly; a couple of the residents also feed the deer.

Bison:

Occasionally bison will be in the parking area for the coffee shop (Kelly on the Gros Ventre). Exercise extreme caution when near bison. They appear slow and lumbering but they can move short distances at 35mph and jump a six-foot fence. Every year a couple of tourists are badly injured by bison.

Site Specific Photography Tips

Mule Deer: Mule deer are relatively tolerant of vehicles. Good images can be obtained from your car window alongside the road.

Bison: When bison are in the parking area or near the roadside, do not exit your car. If they are crossing the road, give them plenty of time to completely clear the roadside. Sit back, enjoy the show, and take pictures from the safety and comfort of your vehicle.

HOTSPOT #10

Meadow north of Kelly to Ditch Creek

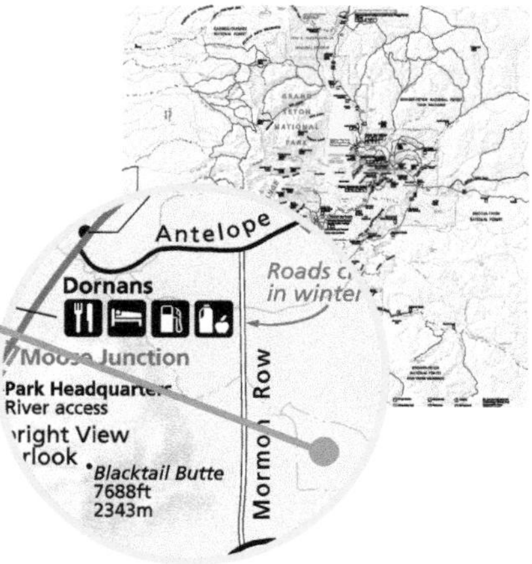

HIGHLIGHTS:

Bison congregate in the meadow from late spring through early autumn. Elk are found in the meadows during spring and fall migration (May and October) and moose forage on bitterbrush in autumn (October-December). Coyotes and foxes are occasionally seen hunting rodents. Raptors, such as short-eared owls, hawks, and eagles also hunt rodents in this area. Sage grouse are a bit elusive but can be seen driving the dirt road that bisects the meadow from Gros Ventre Road to Mormon Row.

DIRECTIONS

Mileage from Jackson Town Square

Travel north on Highway 89 to Gros Ventre Junction (6.9 miles). Turn right on Gros Ventre Road; the meadow begins east of the unpaved Mormon Row (5.1 miles past the junction) and extends to Ditch Creek (16.8 miles).

WILDLIFE IN AREA:

Elk:

Elk use the meadow to forage in autumn and spring, usually when migrating to and from the National Elk Refuge. Early morning and late afternoon provide the best light and lenses in the 300 to 600mm range provide pleasing images. Elk can be a bit skittish, so shooting from your vehicle will yield better frame-filling images.

Coyotes and Foxes:

Predators, such as coyotes and foxes, hunt rodents in this meadow. Both of these predators have interesting pouncing techniques. Coyotes tend to have a long arc-type pounce and foxes tend to have a high arc pounce. Both will look and listen prior to pouncing which will give you time to prepare for a good image.

Mule Deer:

Mule deer occasionally forage near the roadside near the town of Kelly and across from Teton Valley ranch.

Bison:

The meadow is a hotspot for bison from late spring until autumn. Bison forage in the meadow and frequently move between the Elk Ranch Flats (#21) and Kelly area.

Raptors and Sage Grouse:

Most of the raptors are skittish but a 600mm lens can capture some flight shots or images of carcass feeding. Sage grouse are seen on the dirt road that bisects the meadow between Gros Ventre Road and Mormon Row. Beanbag images from the car window are generally best, as the bird will flee when they see a standing human figure.

Moose:

Moose are common in the Kelly-Ditch Creek meadow from October through December. As snow accumulates in the river bottom areas, moose forage the meadow for bitterbrush. Moose are solitary animals; typically, they prefer to be alone, except a cow-calf pair. However, food is very scarce in late autumn and many moose will forage together in this meadow.

MAP 2

Site Specific Photography Tips

Bison: If bison are relatively close, photograph from the protection of your vehicle. Lenses in the 100 to 400mm range work well. If bison are not close (greater than 25 yards), it is relatively safe to photograph from outside your vehicle. Bison are dark animals; good images are possible with the sun at your back but watch for shadows caused by the horns or other obstructions. When snow covers the ground, it provides an excellent reflector to help illuminate these dark animals.

Moose: Lenses in the 300 to 600mm range are best for moose, depending on the distance from the roadside. If near the road, shoot from the protection of your vehicle. If the moose are in an area with the Tetons in the background, switch to a wider lens and smaller aperture (such as f11 or f16) to include the beautiful mountains in your image.

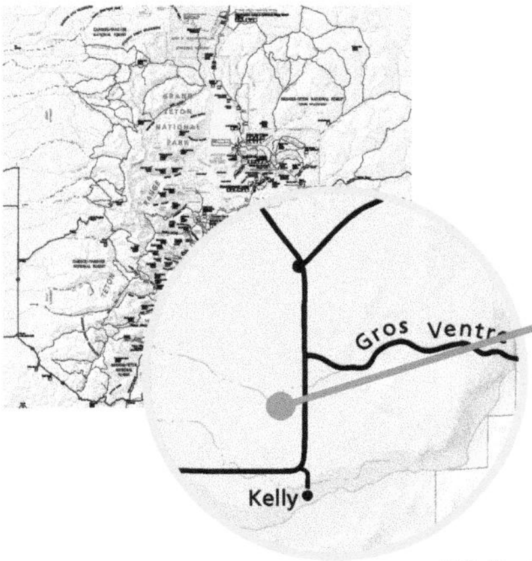

HOTSPOT #11

Kelly Warm Springs and meadow adjacent to Teton Valley Ranch

HIGHLIGHTS:

Like hotspot #10, the Kelly Warm Springs meadow is a prime location for bison and elk. However, moose are an infrequent visitor. Foxes frequently hunt this meadow for rodents; ground squirrels and badgers are occasionally seen near the north bank of the warm spring. Short-eared owls nest and forage this area in late spring-early summer.

DIRECTIONS

Mileage from Jackson Town Square

Travel north on Highway 89 to Gros Ventre Junction (6.9 miles). Turn right on Gros Ventre Road and continue east past Mormon Row (5.1 miles) and the town of Kelly (14.0 miles). Follow the paved road past Kelly as Gros Ventre Road doglegs (Teton Valley Ranch is located at the corner) to the north. Turn right at the next paved road (continuation of Gros Ventre Road), Kelly Warm Springs (15.2 miles) is ahead on the right.

WILDLIFE IN AREA:

Bison and Elk:

This meadow is a frequent location for bison in late spring and occasionally in the summer and autumn. Elk are frequently encountered near Teton Valley Ranch and in the meadow in late spring and early fall.

Moose:

Cow and cow-calf moose are occasionally observed near Kelly Warm Springs whereas bull moose are seen to the east near the aspen trees.

Predators:

Foxes frequently hunt rodents in the meadow near the warm springs. Badger burrows are on the east side of the warm springs, though badgers are rare to see on the bank during the daytime. Short-eared owls nest in the meadow to the south of the warm springs.

MAP 2

Site Specific Photography Tips

Bison and Elk: Late afternoon, when the sun is at your back, is an excellent time to photograph bison and elk in this meadow. Bison also frequent the warm springs area in autumn making interesting images because the cooler air brushing over the warm spring water increases the fog density.

Predators: Badgers are generally nocturnal, though they are more active in springtime when they have young to feed. Foxes are more common in this area in late autumn. Bald eagles perch on the telephone poles near the warm springs area and short-eared owls hunt in the late afternoon; this makes for excellent flight shots.

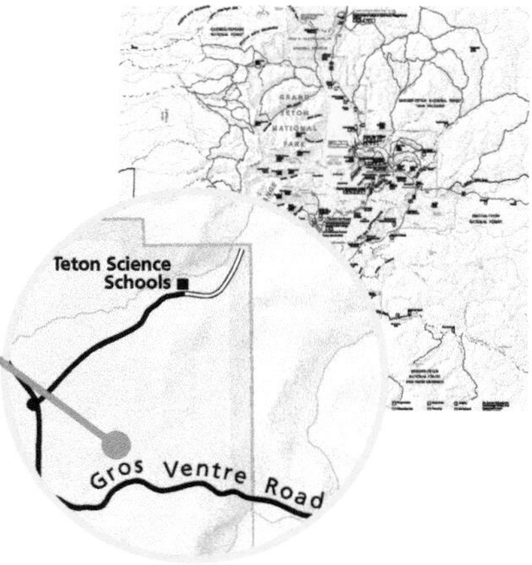

HOTSPOT #12

Shane Cabins to National Forest

HIGHLIGHTS:

The Shane Cabins (Official park name: Luther Taylor Homestead) and surrounding area is good for landscape images. The Gros Ventre landslide and the Red Rock hills are a few miles past the National Forest turnaround; both are good landscape photography locations. Moose frequent the nearby forest during the rut (late September-early October) and the area near the National Forest turnaround in winter. Bull elk congregate on the hillside above the Shane Cabins in early spring and autumn. Foxes also frequent the area around the cabins.

DIRECTIONS

Mileage from Jackson Town Square

Travel north on Highway 89 to Gros Ventre Junction (6.9 miles). Turn right on Gros Ventre Road and continue east past the town of Kelly (14.0 miles). Follow the paved road past Kelly as Gros Ventre Road doglegs to the north. Turn right at the next paved road and continue past Kelly Warm Springs (15.2 miles). Shane Cabins are about a mile up the hill. The park boundary is an additional couple miles further, just before the National Forest turnaround.

WILDLIFE IN AREA:

Moose, Elk, and Foxes:

During winter, moose are frequently seen foraging on willow twigs at the National Forest turnaround. Moose are also found in the aspen forest across from the Shane Cabins near the time of the rut (August through early October). Bull elk are occasionally on the hillside to the east of Shane Cabins when migrating to and from the National Elk Refuge in April-May and November. Foxes hunt the forest and meadow area and are seen traveling the roadside, especially as snow accumulates.

Site Specific Photography Tips

Cabins: The cabins were used in the 1953 Hollywood Western titled *Shane*. A wide-angle lens works well for the cabins with the fencing as a framing element or the mountains as a background.

Animals: At times, animals will be close to the roadside and lenses in the 100-400mm range work well. If you keep your camera adjacent to the driver's seat, you will be ready to capture those fleeting moments as a fox runs up the side of the road or a moose appears on the ridge of the hillside.

MAP 2

HOTSPOT #13

Ditch Creek and meadow at Antelope Flats Road

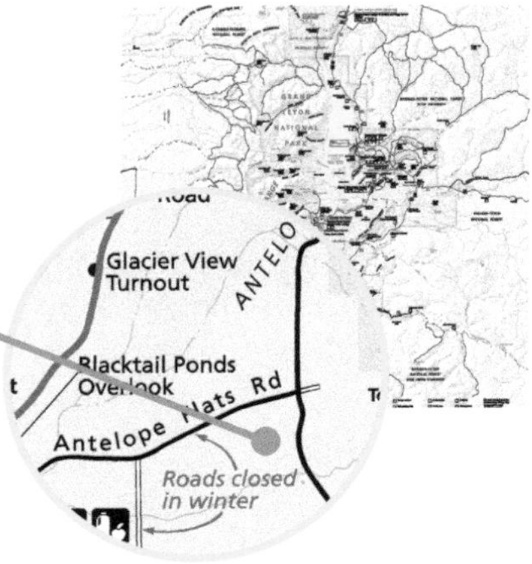

HIGHLIGHTS:

Ditch Creek river bottom is a common location for moose that forage the willows in the drainage area. Porcupines and foxes have also been observed in the area.

DIRECTIONS

Mileage from Jackson Town Square

Travel north on Highway 89 to Gros Ventre Junction (6.9 miles). Turn right on Gros Ventre Road, continue east past the town of Kelly (14.0 miles). The road doglegs to the north and Ditch Creek is an additional couple miles north (16.8 miles).

WILDLIFE IN AREA:

Moose:

The Ditch Creek wetland area and the meadow to the north is a frequent location for moose. Moose forage on the willows and cottonwoods from May through September. However as the snow accumulates, moose forage the meadow for bitterbrush.

Porcupines:

Porcupines occasionally are seen in the cottonwood trees around Ditch Creek and sometimes on the roadside. They can be surprisingly elusive when they encounter humans and will remain stationary if high in a tree.

Foxes:

Red and Cross foxes have been seen in the area foraging for rodents and other prey items. On occasion, they will even den in the area if they find sufficient protection.

Site Specific Photography Tips

Moose: Lenses in the 200 to 600mm range are best for moose, depending on the distance from the roadside. If near the road, shoot from the protection of your vehicle. If the moose are in an area with the Tetons in the background, switch to a wider depth of field (such as f11 or f16) to include the beautiful mountains in your image.

Porcupine and Fox: If you have your camera exposure setting preset, you will increase your chances of getting nice images of these critters. Both can move quickly from the roadside. When porcupines are in the trees, it can be a challenge to get a clean background but they will generally remain stationary if you do not approach closer than the roadside. A long lens on a tripod can be moved about to get a more pleasing background.

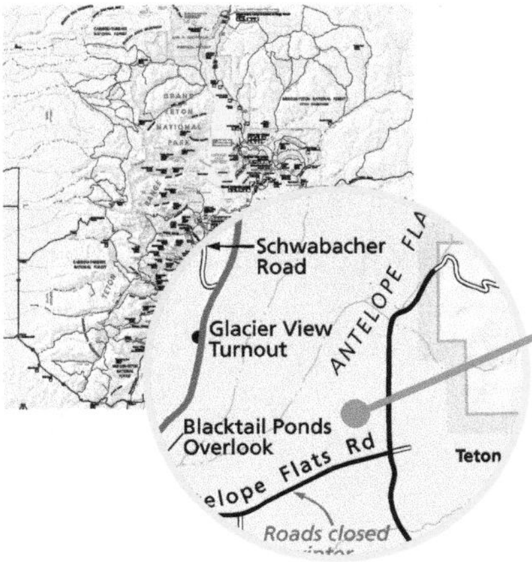

HOTSPOT #14

Mailbox Corner to National Forest

HIGHLIGHTS:

Where Antelope Flats Road doglegs west toward Mormon Row, the corner at the dogleg is known as Mailbox Corner as that was the location of mailboxes for Mormon Row many years ago. The lower Gros Ventre wolf pack is frequently viewed near the older cabins from late autumn through early spring. Bison frequently cross this area toward Mormon Row.

DIRECTIONS

Mileage from Jackson Town Square

Travel north on Highway 89 to Gros Ventre Junction (6.9 miles). Turn right on Gros Ventre Road and continue east past the town of Kelly (14.0 miles). Follow Gros Ventre Road as it doglegs to the north. Mailbox Corner (17.6 miles) and the National Forest access (19.1 miles) are ahead to the north.

WILDLIFE IN AREA:

MAP 2

Wolves:

Wolves are generally very elusive. They typically hunt between late evening and early morning. Occasionally, wolves are seen bedded down west of the cabins that are north of Mailbox Corner.

Bison:

Bison migrate frequently from Elk Ranch to Mormon Row. Generally, they will move as a herd and in a linear row. Exercise caution with bison, as they appear slow and lumbering but they can move very quickly.

Site Specific Photography Tips

Wolves: Wolves are elusive; close up images of wolves are difficult because they typically avoid areas near humans. Lenses in the 500 to 600mm range are useful but you must always have your exposure preset and be ready for a quick shot out the vehicle window. Patience is a real virtue for wolves; some photographers wait ten hours a day, for weeks, for one image.

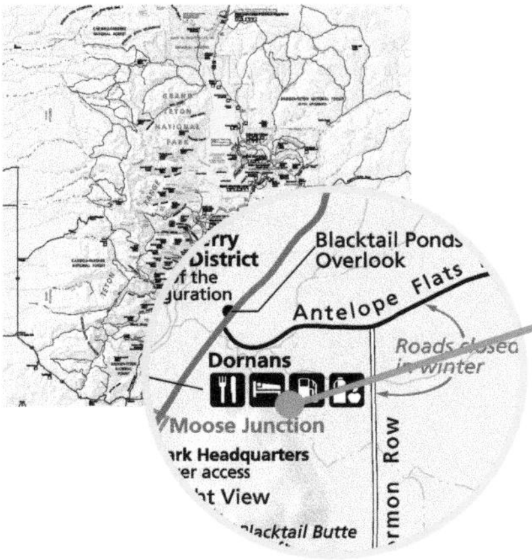

HOTSPOT #15

Mormon Row

HIGHLIGHTS:

Bison frequent the Mormon Row area from late spring through early autumn. Occasionally coyotes, badgers, and weasels are seen in the area. Uinta ground squirrels are nearly ubiquitous near the Pink House and John Moulton barn from late spring until early autumn. Songbirds, such as mountain bluebirds and western meadowlarks, are common in the aspens and on the fence posts.

DIRECTIONS

Mileage from Jackson Town Square

Travel north on Highway 89 to Gros Ventre Junction (6.9 miles). Turn right on Gros Ventre Road and turn north onto Mormon Row (12.0 miles). The dirt road is bumpy but a good area to observe wildlife. Alternately, continue on Gros Ventre Road past Kelly to Mailbox Corner (17.6 miles). Turn left and proceed west for 1.7 miles (19.3 miles) to Mormon Row. The Pink House and John Moulton barn are on your right, the bed and breakfast plus other houses and barns are to your left.

MAP 2

WILDLIFE IN AREA:

Uinta Ground Squirrels:

Ground squirrels live in burrows and forage for grasses and flowers. These squirrels are relatively tame because of human presence in the area. Uinta ground squirrels hibernate from late August through early April. Soon after emerging from their winter hibernation, they mate and have a bevy of babies in May.

Predators:

Coyotes, badgers, weasels, and raptors frequent the area to feast on the ground squirrel population. Despite the number of ground squirrels, these predators are seen relatively infrequently.

Bison:

Bison are occasionally seen near the barns and houses. Exercise caution around these huge creatures because they can move at speeds of 35mph and jump a six-foot fence.

Birds:

Mountain bluebirds and western meadowlarks are frequent visitors from spring through autumn. Sage grouse live in the sagebrush meadows. A sage grouse lek is located to the north of the John Moulton barn; the lek is active in April and the beginning of May.

Site Specific Photography Tips

Bison: On occasion, bison are near the John Moulton barn in the morning providing an opportunity to get bison, the barn and the Tetons in one image. If you desire the mountains and bison to both be sharp, use a smaller aperture (such as f11 or f16).

Ground Squirrel: Lenses in the 100 to 400mm range will be sufficient for ground squirrels. Getting low to the ground provides a pleasing perspective. With a little patience, you will also capture images of the squirrels standing on their hind legs, maybe eating a flower or calling to their mates.

HOTSPOT #16

Blacktail Ponds

MAP 2

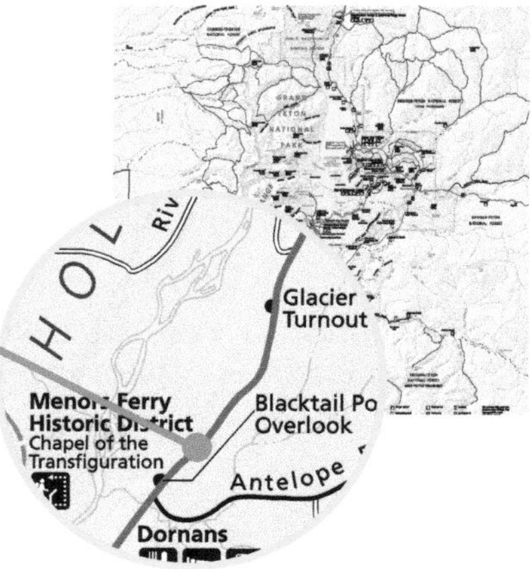

HIGHLIGHTS:

Blacktail Ponds overlooks the Snake River drainage with moose and elk in the wetland areas from May through early winter (November-December). Grouse, soras, and other birds are common in the area. Blacktail Ponds is also an excellent landscape photography location.

DIRECTIONS

Mileage from Jackson Town Square

Travel north on Highway 89 past Gros Ventre Junction, Moose Junction, and Antelope Flats Junction. Blacktail Ponds is the next road (13.9 miles). Turn left and follow to parking area.

WILDLIFE IN AREA:

Moose and Elk:

Moose and elk frequent the Blacktail Pond area from spring through autumn. Moose are near the ponds just northwest of the parking area, whereas elk are frequently farther to the north in the drainage area. During the rut, the bull elk come into the area in search of females. Many times, you will hear the bull elk bugling during the rut before you see them.

Site Specific Photography Tips

Moose and Elk: Lenses in the 200 to 600mm range are best for moose and elk. However, wide-angle lenses are helpful if the moose are in the ponds at sunset. The Tetons are to the west, providing a dramatic backdrop.

HOTSPOT #17

Schwabacher Landing

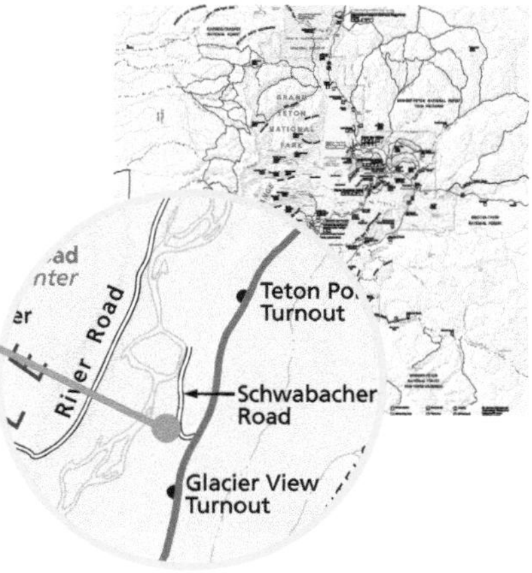

HIGHLIGHTS:

Of the premier landscape locations in the Tetons, Schwabacher Landing tops the list. An early morning sunrise landscape outing is an almost guaranteed wall image. Animals that frequent the area include moose, beaver, badger, weasel, squirrel, chipmunk, and waterfowl. As you drive down the access road to Schwabacher Landing, there is a turnout near the bottom of the hill and a larger parking area at the bottom of the hill. This first turnout is a good location for beavers and some waterfowl and the main parking area is great for landscapes plus additional animals.

DIRECTIONS

Mileage from Jackson Town Square

Travel north on Highway 89 (past Gros Ventre Junction, Moose Junction, and Antelope Flats Junction to Schwabacher Landing (8.5 miles), turn left. Go 1.0 mile to the first turn or to the end of the drive to the parking area.

WILDLIFE IN AREA:

Moose:

Moose are seldom at the first turnout. Head to the parking area at the end of the driveway. Follow the walkway northward adjacent to the river to a relatively large pond. Moose are frequently in this area and infrequently along the path toward this pond.

MAP 2

Beaver:

Beavers are also abundant at Schwabacher Landing and they are most active dawn and dusk. You will see them swimming in the ponds, building on the dams and lodges and occasionally standing on the shoreline.

Squirrels and Chipmunks:

Ground squirrels are abundant and there are also a few tree-dwelling squirrels in the area. Least chipmunks are common and can be a bit friendly.

Waterfowl:

Goldeneye and mallard ducks are common in the area; other species of ducks, coots, etc., also use the water areas for feeding. Most of the year, these ducks are tame but during hunting season (autumn), they become very elusive.

Badgers and Weasels:

Badgers and weasels are common enough to be an occasional sighting. Badgers are most active at night but you will see their oval-shaped burrows. Weasels are more active than badgers during the day but difficult to photograph as they seldom remain still.

Site Specific Photography Tips

Moose: Many times, you will see moose nearly hidden in the conifer trees behind the ponds. If you are patient, many times they will come into the water to feed on aquatic plants. Aquatic plants have more sodium content and this is an essential mineral in their diet. Lenses in the 100 to 600mm range are more than sufficient for moose in this area. The Teton Range forms a beautiful backdrop, so remember to use a wider lens and small aperture (f11 or f16) for images to include moose and the Tetons in the same shot.

Beaver: Water mammals look their best in the softer light at dawn and dusk. Also, they tend to have lower contrast in deep overcast light. The color of early morning light on the pond surface contrasts well with the swimming beavers. Lenses in the 400 to 600mm range are best for beavers unless they happen to come close.

Map #3

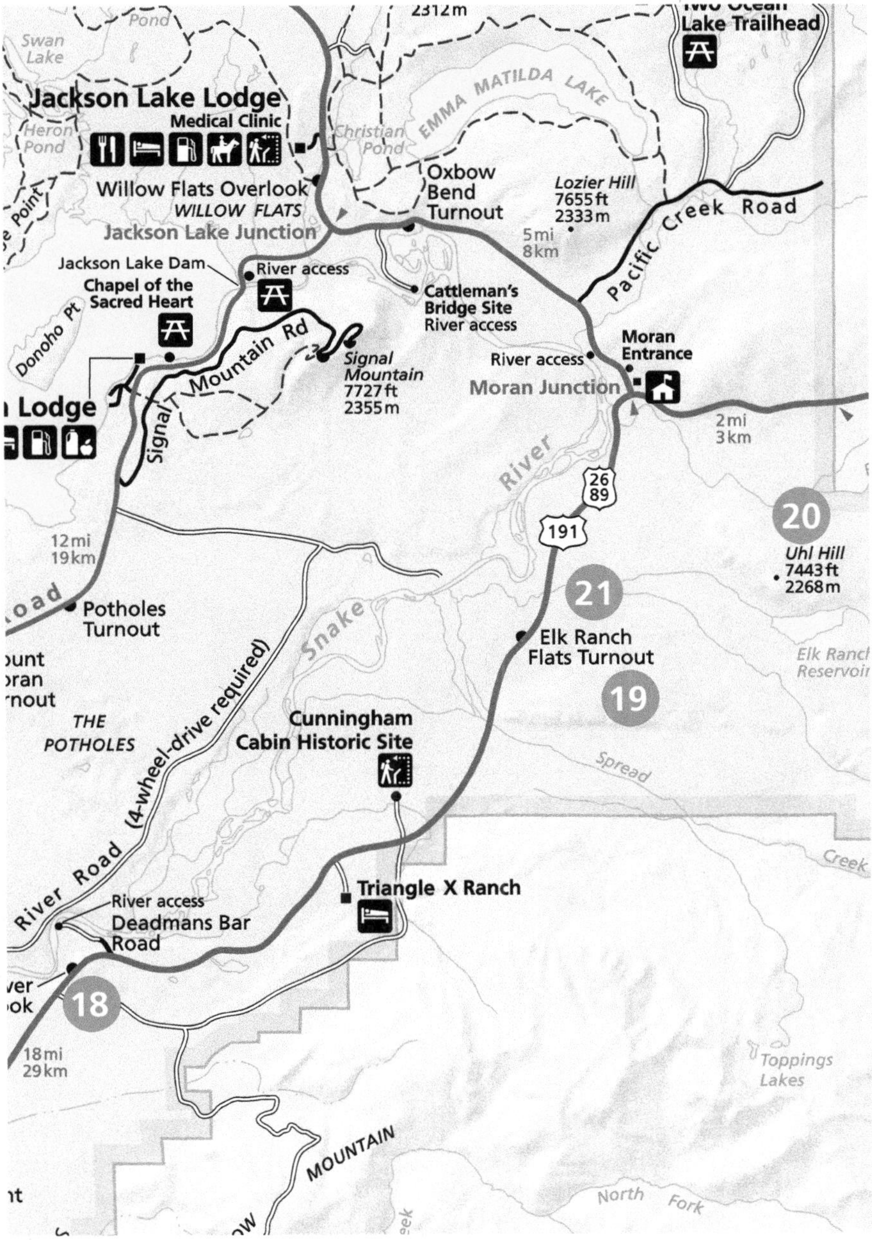
Two Ocean Lake Trailhead
Swan Lake
Pond
Jackson Lake Lodge
Medical Clinic
Heron Pond
Christian Pond
EMMA MATILDA LAKE
Willow Flats Overlook
WILLOW FLATS
Jackson Lake Junction
Oxbow Bend Turnout
Lozier Hill
7655 ft
2333 m
5 mi
8 km
Pacific Creek Road
Jackson Lake Dam
River access
Chapel of the Sacred Heart
Cattleman's Bridge Site
River access
Donoho Pt
Signal Mountain Rd
Signal Mountain
7727 ft
2355 m
River access
Moran Entrance
Moran Junction
Lodge
2 mi
3 km
River
26
89
191
20
Uhl Hill
7443 ft
2268 m
12 mi
19 km
Road
Potholes Turnout
21
Snake
Elk Ranch Flats Turnout
Elk Ranch Reservoir
19
THE POTHOLES
River Road (4-wheel-drive required)
Cunningham Cabin Historic Site
Spread
Creek
Triangle X Ranch
River access
Deadmans Bar Road
18
18 mi
29 km
Toppings Lakes
MOUNTAIN
North Fork

HOTSPOT #18

Snake River Overlook

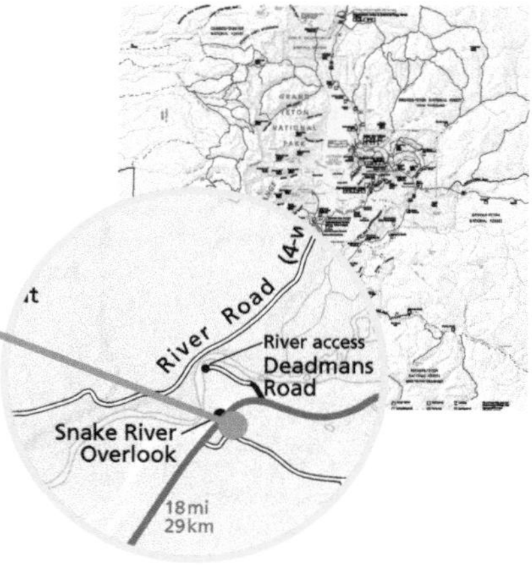

HIGHLIGHTS:

Ansel Adams photographed his famous "Tetons and Snake River" image from this location in 1942. Snake River Overlook is primarily a landscape photography location, however, there is a red fox that is commonly seen in the area begging for handouts.

DIRECTIONS

Mileage from Jackson Town Square

Travel north on Highway 89 (past Gros Ventre Junction, Moose Junction, Antelope Flats Junction, and Schwabacher Landing). Snake River Overlook is ahead on the left, turn left into the parking area (21.1 miles).

WILDLIFE IN AREA:

Elk:

When elk are migrating to and from the National Elk Refuge in April-May and November-December, it is common to see them from the overlook area by the Snake River or to the east in the sagebrush meadows.

Fox:

It is illegal to feed the wildlife in a national park. However, there is a fox commonly seen at the Snake River Overlook parking area, especially in winter when the snow is deep. The park service keeps a portion of the parking area plowed for visitor traffic.

Site Specific Photography Tips

Ansel Adams captured one of his most famous images from this location but the river course has changed slightly since that time. However, this is still an excellent location for landscape images. Use a wide-angle lens at dawn, dusk, or during inclement weather to capture a dramatic view of the foreground and mountains.

Foxes: Foxes also frequent this area begging for snacks. A 100 to 400mm lens is usually sufficient to capture nice fox images in this area. If you are lucky, a fox will stand on the stone wall or a snow bank with the mountains in the background.

HOTSPOT #19

Wolf Ranch Road

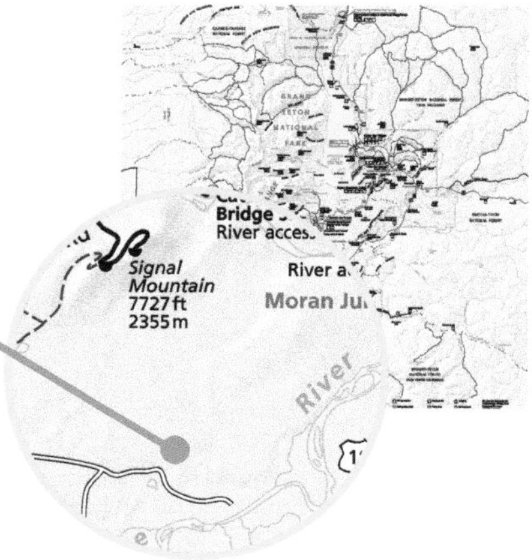

HIGHLIGHTS:

Wolf Ranch Road borders the southern edge of Elk Ranch Flats. A couple log-cabin type houses and two ranch houses are located on the road. Bison, pronghorn, hawks, ground squirrels, and badgers are frequently encountered along this stretch of road. On occasion, grizzly bears and owls are also seen in the area.

DIRECTIONS

Mileage from Jackson Town Square

Travel north on Highway 89 past Triangle X Dude Ranch and Moosehead Ranch; Wolf Ranch Road is on the right (27.2 miles) just prior to Elk Ranch. Turn right onto the dirt road. A four-wheel drive may be needed for some areas. Wolf Ranch Road is 2.1 miles long before it joins Uhl Hill Road just after the cattle guard.

WILDLIFE IN AREA:

Pronghorn:

Pronghorn are frequently seen in open areas of the meadows north of the road. Pronghorn are North America's fastest mammal with excellent eyesight; they can avoid most predators by staying in unobstructed open areas. Pronghorns migrate south (to the area near Pinedale, Wyoming) as the snow accumulates but return to the area as the snow abates.

Bison:

Bison are frequently seen north of the road in the meadows and south on the hillside. Bison naturally move about from one foraging location to another. They travel south across the hillside to the meadows of Antelope Flats and Kelly (#11 and 13). They also venture east to the meadows near Uhl Hill (#20).

MAP 3

Ground Squirrels, Raptors and Badgers:

Uinta ground squirrels are abundant near the roadside from April through August. Because of their abundance, raptors, and badgers are also common. The raptors generally are most abundant east of the two ranch houses. Badgers burrow into the hillside on the south side of the road. They are most active at night but have been seen digging for rodents or walking on the hillside and meadows in the daytime. Great gray owls have also been spotted along the roadside near Highway 89.

Site Specific Photography Tips

Bison: Bison range from close to far away in the flats. When closer, lenses in the 300 to 600mm range provide frame-filling images. In May, bison babies ('red dogs") are birthed; these young bison are photogenic. Dandelions and other wildflowers are abundant in late May and early June; these provide an attractive punch of color for your bison images.

Pronghorn: Pronghorn generally are found in small herds of three to five does and a single buck will generally be nearby. They generally give birth to single or twin fawns in late May. Lenses in the 400 to 600mm range are generally best to capture them as they can be skittish.

Hawk: The hawks perch high in the cottonwood trees to the south of the road and fly over the meadows for food. Flight shots with a 300 to 600mm lens are possible as the hawks forage.

Great gray owl: Owls tend to perch in trees during the daytime and forage in the evenings and overnight. Beautiful images of owls perched next to the rough cottonwood bark can be obtained with lenses in the 400 to 600mm range. Flight shots from this area are rare but always be prepared for the unexpected.

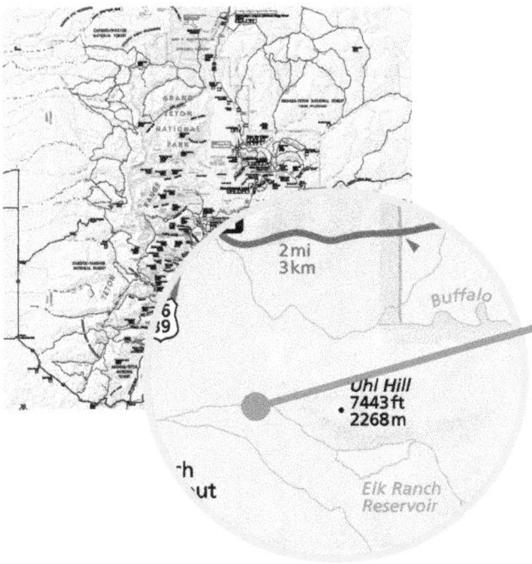

HOTSPOT #20

Uhl Hill

MAP 3

HIGHLIGHTS:

Bison are common in the meadows below Uhl Hill. Golden eagles nest on the upper hillside and wolves den in the area. On occasion, coyotes are seen in the meadows.

DIRECTIONS

Mileage from Jackson Town Square

Travel north on Highway 89 past Triangle X Dude Ranch and Moosehead Ranch to Wolf Ranch Road (27.2 miles). Turn right on Wolf Ranch Road and travel 2.1 miles before it joins Uhl Hill Road just after the cattle guard. Make a right turn after the cattle guard and fence; Uhl Hill Road winds around for many miles adjacent to the hillside and through the sagebrush meadows.

WILDLIFE IN AREA:

Bison:

Bison forage the meadows adjacent to Uhl Hill. As winter snow abates, bison move into this area from the National Elk Refuge because the snow density is less.

Wolves and Coyotes:

The sagebrush is dense in the meadows making it difficult to see wolves and coyotes. Using binoculars or a spotting scope, occasionally you will spot wolves on this hillside.

Golden Eagles:

Golden eagles nest in the open caves on Uhl Hill and forage in the meadows. The nests are beyond the range of normal telephone lenses, though good flight shots are possible as the eagles forage the meadows.

Site Specific Photography Tips

Bison, wolves, eagles, etc: The meadows of Uhl Hill are so open that most photography in the area is best from the vehicle. Very little traffic ventures into this area, providing many hours of solitude with the animals and your camera. Lenses in the 100 to 400mm range work well in this area because the animals tend to be near the dirt road.

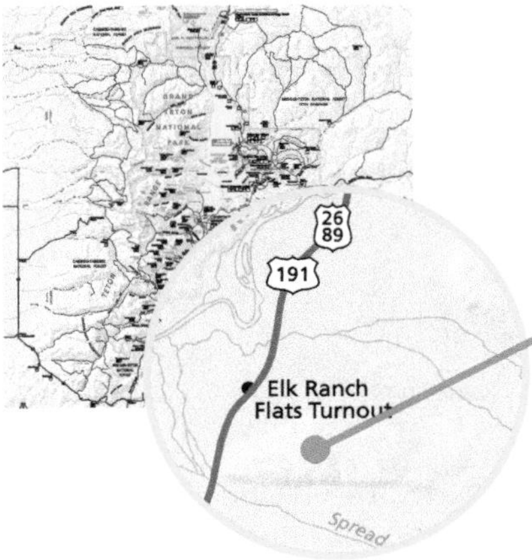

HOTSPOT #21

Elk Ranch Flats

HIGHLIGHTS:

Bison, pronghorn, and elk frequent Elk Ranch Flats from late spring through early autumn. Grizzly bears are occasionally seen, especially if a large mammal carcass is present. Coyotes are seen hunting in the flats year-around.

DIRECTIONS

Mileage from Jackson Town Square

Travel north on Highway 89 past Cunningham Cabin (25.2 miles), Triangle X Dude Ranch, and Moosehead Ranch. Elk Ranch Flats borders both sides of Highway 89 for a couple miles (27.7-29.7 miles).

WILDLIFE IN AREA:

Pronghorn:

Pronghorn are frequently seen in groups of three to five individuals in the open areas of the meadows. Occasionally they are close to the highway.

Bison:

Throughout late spring to early autumn, bison are frequently seen in the east and west meadows, occasionally crossing Highway 89.

Coyotes:

Coyotes are frequent visitors to the flats year-around. They typically hunt for rodents in the flats, occasionally close enough for nice images.

Elk and Bears:

Elk are seen early spring and late autumn during the migration to and from the National Elk Refuge. Grizzly bears are also occasionally seen in the flats, especially in spring and autumn when they feed on dandelions and ground squirrels. When the bears first emerge from hibernation, they will frequently check the flats for winter bison carcasses. Some bison that do not migrate to the elk refuge die of starvation because the deep snow makes obtaining food difficult.

MAP 3

Site Specific Photography Tips

Bison: Bison range from close to far away in the flats. When closer, lenses in the 300 to 600mm range provide frame-filling images. In May, bison babies ('red dogs") are born.

Pronghorn: Pronghorn, North America's fastest mammal, have a beautiful tan and white coat. Lenses in the 400 to 600mm range are generally best to capture them as they can be a bit skittish.

Coyote: Traffic along Highway 89 can be heavy and coyotes in this area are accustomed to vehicles. People also stop frequently to view the bison, elk, and pronghorn. Lenses in the 300 to 600mm range are sufficient when the coyotes venture close to the roadside.

Map #4

COVERING HOTSPOTS #22-24

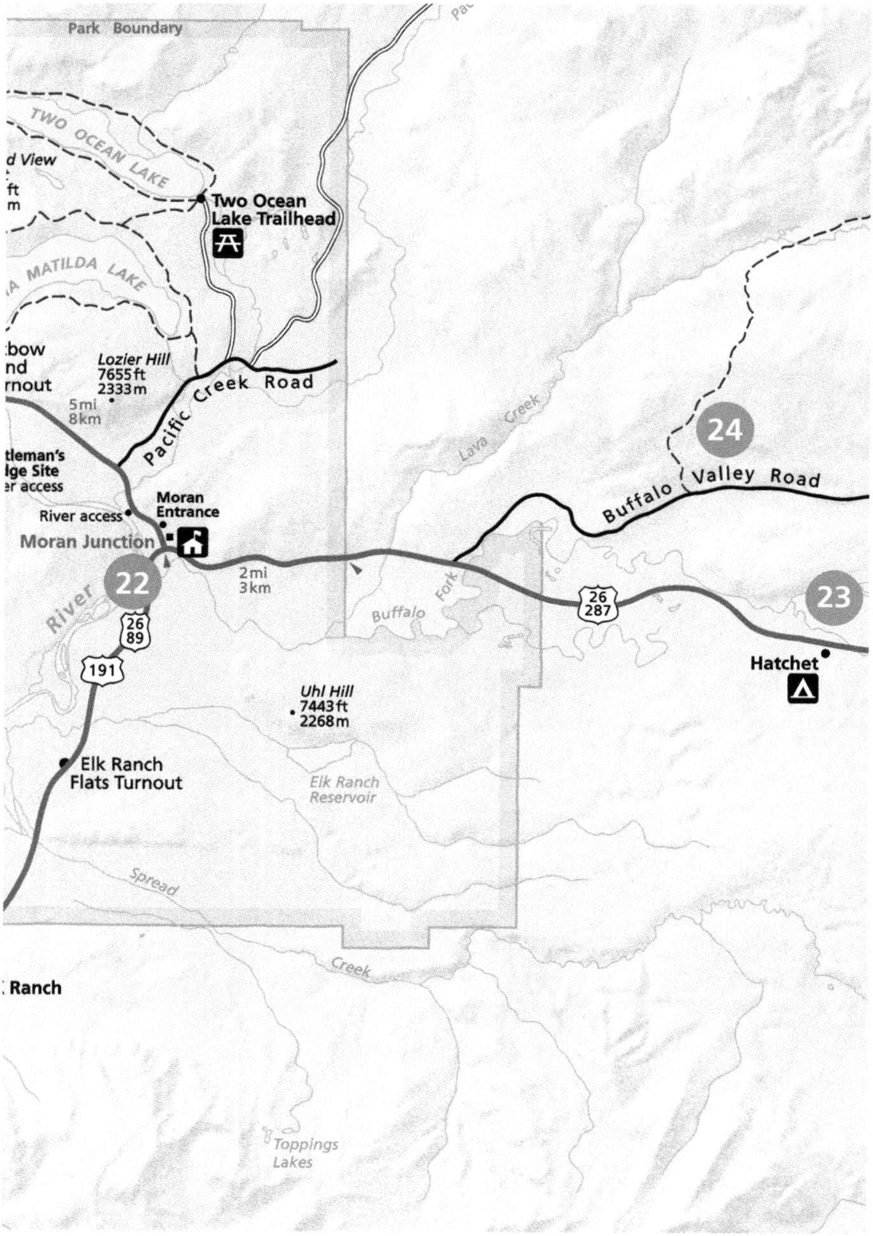

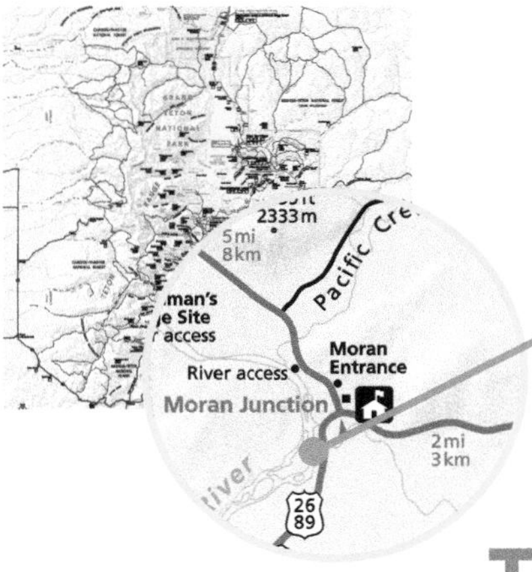

HOTSPOT #22

Moran Junction to Togwotee Lodge

MAP 4

HIGHLIGHTS:

The seventeen miles stretch between Moran Junction and Togwotee Lodge is a hotspot for grizzly bears. Wolves are frequently encountered between Moran Junction and Fireside Resort. Elk and moose frequent the area but are seldom close enough for good images.

DIRECTIONS

Mileage from Jackson Town Square

Travel north on Highway 89 to Moran Junction (30.8 miles). At Moran Junction, continue east on Highway 26 toward Dubois. As you head toward Dubois, you will pass Buffalo Valley Road, Fireside Resort, an entrance to Turpin Meadow, and Togwotee Lodge (47.6 miles).

WILDLIFE IN AREA:

Grizzly Bears:

Bears frequent the hillsides and meadows along the roadside in spring foraging on dandelions. Later in the summer and early autumn, bears are feasting on the occasional moose or elk carcass.

Wolves:

Wolves are occasional visitors during winter and early spring. In early spring, the cattle on the ranches are calving. Wolves visit the area for the cattle birthing in spring to predate on the newborn calves.

Site Specific Photography Tips

Grizzly Bears: This section is outside the park and the protection of National Park rangers. Some may be tempted to approach bears closer than is safe. The safety of yourself and the bears should be your primary concern. Lenses in the 500 to 600mm range are the best option. Teleconverters are a valuable accessory to extend your reach. At times, close approach is possible but resist the temptation, as bears are fast and quick. Because the highway runs east-west, the sun angle will be favorable in the morning and late afternoon. However, midday images are also possible as the bears forage on the north hillside.

Wolves: Because of the elusive nature of wolves, have your camera preset for possible wolf encounters. Occasionally, the wolves are crossing the highway or hiding in the willows by the roadside.

MAP 4

HOTSPOT #23

Dubois

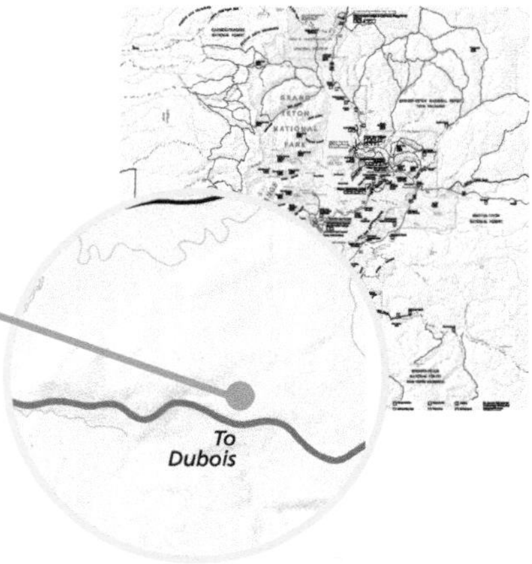

HIGHLIGHTS:

The Whiskey Mountain area of Dubois hosts one of the nation's largest concentration of bighorn sheep. Mule deer are also common in the area. Occasionally bears, wolves, and various birds visit the area.

DIRECTIONS

Mileage from Jackson Town Square

Travel north on Highway 89 past Moran Junction (30.8 miles) and over the pass to Dubois. The Bighorn Sheep Center is in the heart of Dubois. The Whiskey Basin Wildlife Habitat Area is an additional 4.5 miles east of town. Turn right on Trail Forest Road (also known as Forest Road #411). Stay to the left fork and continue on the road a couple miles to the viewing kiosk. A couple miles past the kiosk is an open meadow bordered by the mountains that hosts the sheep.

WILDLIFE IN AREA:

Bighorn Sheep:

Because of deep winter snowfall, bighorn sheep spend the winter months, roughly November through April, in the valley of the Whiskey Mountains near Dubois. The bighorn sheep rut is near the second week of December. During the rut, rams compete for the ewes with "bone cracking" head blows. Rams are seldom hurt by the head butting but it is an impressive sight.

Mule Deer:

Mule deer are also common in the Whiskey Mountain valley, especially as the snow accumulates in the high country. Herds of fifteen to twenty individuals are not unusual but trophy bucks are seldom seen.

Bears, Wolves, and Birds:

Bears and wolves are infrequently seen in the area. However, have your camera ready on the seat. If you have your exposure preset, you will be ready for that fleeting encounter.

Site Specific Photography Tips

Bighorn Sheep: Ewes, lambs, and rams will be in the meadow areas during the daytime but will head into the higher mountain area from late afternoon through early morning. When possible, try to photograph the sheep with the red rocks in the background for a dynamic image. Use a wide aperture (f5.6 or f7.1) to render the red rocks out of focus or use a narrow aperture to include the cliffs as a compositional element.

Mule Deer: Like the bighorn sheep, mule deer look dramatic against the red rock cliffs, either with a wide aperture to throw the background out of focus or a narrow aperture to include the cliffs as a compositional element.

HOTSPOT #24

Buffalo Valley Road

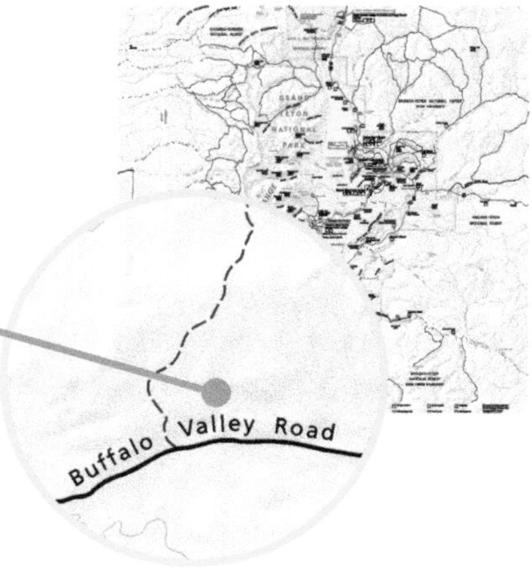

MAP 4

HIGHLIGHTS:

Fox, mule deer, grizzly bears, elk, and moose are common along stretches of Buffalo Fork Road. Elk, mule deer, grizzly bears, and fox are more common on the uplands to the north and moose are more common in the wetland areas to the south. Trumpeter swans, nesting osprey, and other waterfowl are common in late spring (May-June) along the Buffalo Fork between Highway 26 and the Heart Six Ranch. Swallows nest under the Turpin Meadow ranch bridge.

DIRECTIONS

Mileage from Jackson Town Square

Travel north on Highway 89 to Moran Junction (30.8 miles). At Moran Junction, continue east on Highway 26 for a couple miles. Buffalo Valley Road is located just east of the Buffalo Fork River. The road is 14.5 miles long and winds among the uplands and lowlands of the Buffalo Valley. After you exit Highway 26, Heart Six Ranch will be on the left as the road turns from north to east; Turpin Meadow Ranch will be at the next major bend in the road as you head toward Highway 26.

WILDLIFE IN AREA:

Grizzly Bears:

Photographic opportunities are possible as the bears descend the north slope toward the lower wetland areas. In some sections, the trees and brush border the road closely; this provides hiding places for animals but also increases the danger. Always carry bear spray in this area and have it ready for immediate use.

Fox:

Foxes are typically encountered in the upland area between Heart Six Ranch and the Turpin Meadow Ranch. In winter, they are more common along the roadside as snow becomes deep in the uplands.

Osprey, Trumpeter Swans and Waterfowl:

Buffalo Fork Road is one of the few places where it is possible to photograph osprey nests from above. The nests are located on tall poles in the river bottoms and the road is constructed on the higher ground of the upland areas. Other waterfowl are difficult to photograph unless you descend the steep slopes to the water's edge.

Mule Deer, Elk, and Moose:

Mule deer and elk are frequently encountered on the upland slopes and forest regions to the north of the road. Deer and elk are most active in mornings and late afternoon. Because of wolves and bears in the area, deer and elk typically stay under the canopy tree area unless actively feeding in the meadow. Moose prefer the wetland areas.

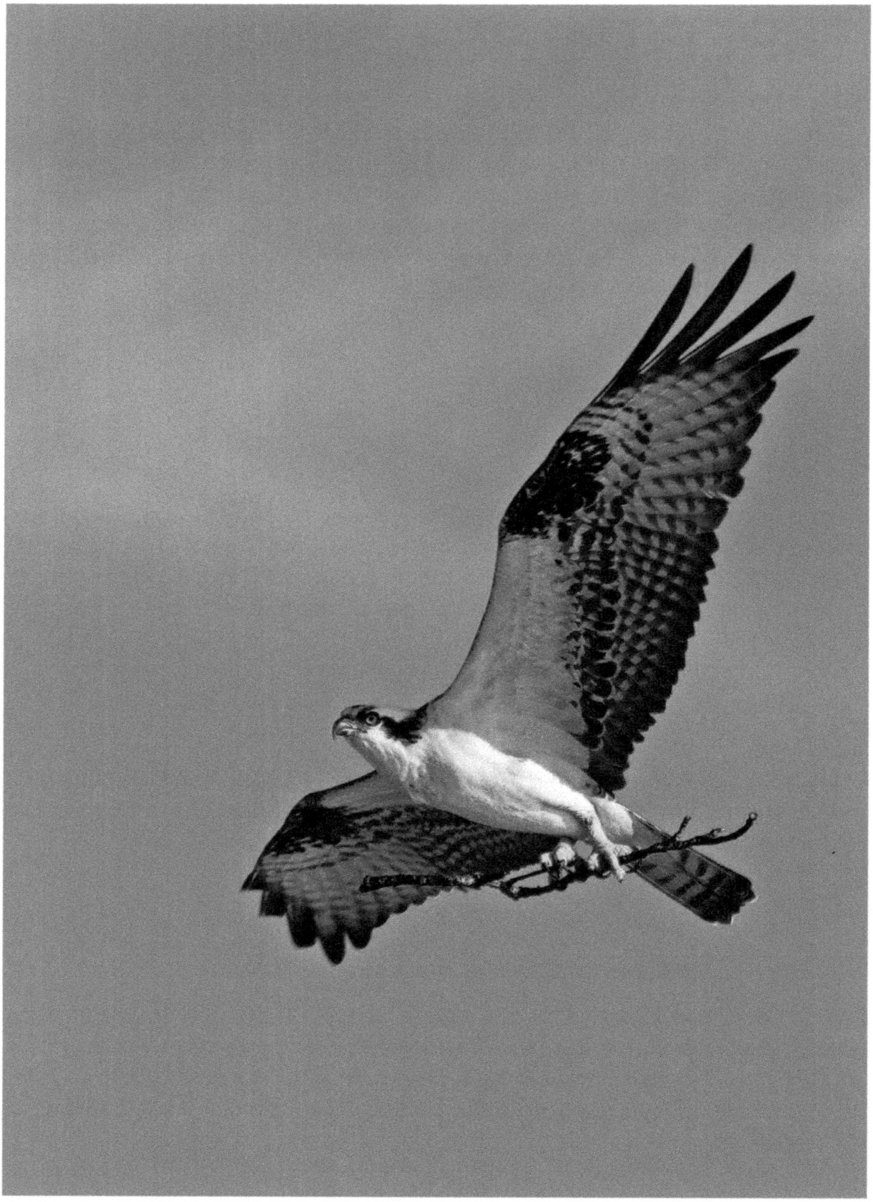

MAP 4

Site Specific Photography Tips

Deer, Elk, and Moose: Animals are frequently close to the road making frame-filling images possible with moderate to long telephoto lenses. However, photography can be challenging because of dappled light through the tree canopy. If you wait until the animal moves to the meadows or clearing, beautiful images are possible.

COVERING HOTSPOTS #25-33

Map #5

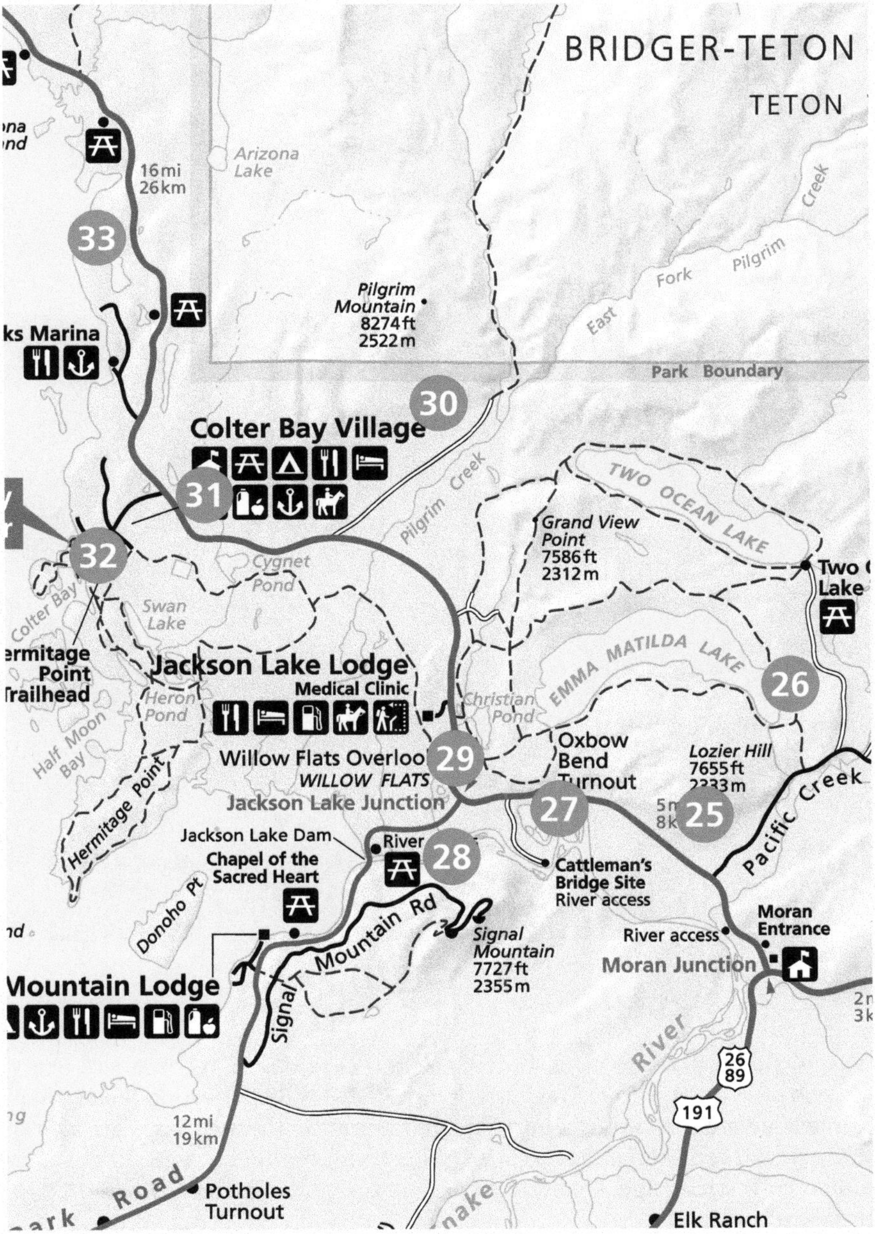
BRIDGER-TETON
TETON
Arizona Lake
16 mi 26 km
33
Pilgrim Mountain 8274 ft 2522 m
East Fork Pilgrim Creek
Park Boundary
ks Marina
30
Colter Bay Village
31
Pilgrim Creek
32
Cygnet Pond
Swan Lake
Colter Bay
Two Ocean Lake
Grand View Point 7586 ft 2312 m
Emma Matilda Lake
26
ermitage Point Trailhead
Jackson Lake Lodge
Medical Clinic
Heron Pond
Christian Pond
Half Moon Bay
Willow Flats Overloo
29
Oxbow Bend Turnout
Lozier Hill 7655 ft
WILLOW FLATS
Jackson Lake Junction
27
25
Pacific Creek
Hermitage Point
Jackson Lake Dam
River
28
Chapel of the Sacred Heart
Cattleman's Bridge Site River access
Signal Mountain Rd
Signal Mountain 7727 ft 2355 m
Donoho Pt
River access
Moran Entrance
Moran Junction
Mountain Lodge
River
26 89
191
12 mi 19 km
Road
Potholes Turnout
Elk Ranch

HOTSPOT #25

Pacific Creek Road and Lozier Hill

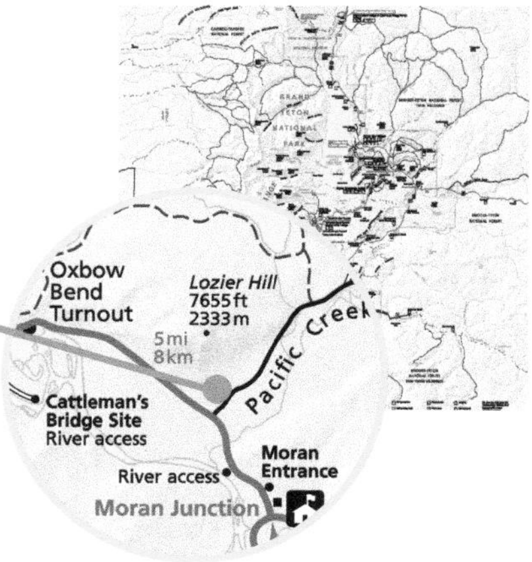

HIGHLIGHTS:

Grizzly and black bears are commonly seen on the slopes of Lozier Hill. Bears are also seen along Pacific Creek Road from Highway 89 to beyond the Braman Homestead area. Elk, wolves, and pine martens are in the area from late spring through early autumn (May-October). Moose visit the willow areas at the overlook near the roadside. Foxes, coyotes, and ground squirrels are common in the meadows.

DIRECTIONS

Mileage from Jackson Town Square

Travel north on Highway 89 to Moran Junction, turn left and go through the park gate; continue Highway 89 to Pacific Creek Road (32.0 miles). Turn right on Pacific Creek Road (Lozier Hill is to the left). Travel down Pacific Creek Road passing the overlook and Two Ocean Road. Pacific Creek Road doglegs to the left. Follow the dogleg for 3.9 miles to National Forest access. The dogleg section travels through very beautiful wildflower meadows, aspen islands, and mixed conifer forests. If you continue straight at the dog-leg, the access road continues to the Braman Homestead on Pacific Creek (34.2 miles). The Braman Homestead is a private housing development and access into the homestead is restricted.

WILDLIFE IN AREA:

Wolves and Pine Martens:

Wolves are elusive animals but are occasionally seen in the area in early mornings and evenings. Pine martens have been observed near the Braman Homestead in the pine forest canopy. Have your camera on the seat next to you as you drive, as you might be able to get a shot of a wolf or pine marten before they duck for cover.

Bears:

Grizzly and black bears are seen in Pacific Creek area from late April to June and again in late September into October. They frequently cross from the Oxbow Bend-Pacific Creek area to Emma Matilda and Two Ocean lakes to the east.

Foxes, Coyotes and Ground Squirrels:

Ground squirrels emerge from hibernation in April providing a prey source for the resident coyotes and foxes. At times, the predators will also den in the area in the downed trees and other natural dens.

Elk and Moose:

Elk are common on the hillside and meadows in mornings and evenings from May through October. Moose are in the wetland areas adjacent to Pacific Creek and the various drainage areas near the creek.

Site Specific Photography Tips

Bears: Bears frequent the slopes of Lozier Hill and eventually come into the meadows and occasionally cross the roads. Lenses in the range of 400 to 600mm provide dynamic images when the bears come into the meadows.

Elk and Moose: Lenses in the 300 to 600mm range are good for moose and elk when they are in the meadows and willow areas. When the elk are under the forest canopy, the dappled light can sometimes present problems with dynamic range and shadows.

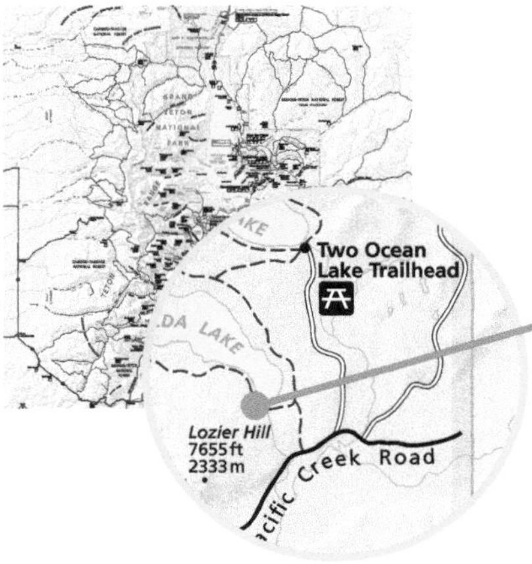

HOTSPOT #26

Two Ocean Lake Road

HIGHLIGHTS:

Bears are relatively common in the lake area and along the road approaching the lake. Coyotes, foxes, elk, and moose are also frequently seen along the road. Two Ocean Lake is also a beautiful spot for landscape and flower pictures. Two Ocean Lake and nearby Emma Matilda Lake are excellent locations for hikes to view the wildflowers and scenery. Make sure to carry bear spray.

DIRECTIONS

Mileage from Jackson Town Square

Travel north on Highway 89 for 30.8 miles. Turn left at Moran Junction and proceed to Pacific Creek Road (32.0 miles). Turn right on Pacific Creek Road and continue past the overlook until you reach Two Ocean Road (32.9 miles). Turn left on Two Ocean. A four-wheel or high-clearance vehicle may be required during the rainy periods. Two Ocean Road winds through the willows, mixed conifer forest, aspen islands, and wildflower meadows for 2.4 miles before dead-ending at the parking area for Two Ocean Lake.

WILDLIFE IN AREA:

Bears:

Grizzly and black bears forage the lakeshore for fish. They also forage the forest and meadows for plant material and critters. Many times, the forest edge approaches the roadside, so be very careful if exiting your vehicle and carry bear spray for protection from an unexpected encounter.

Coyotes, Foxes, Elk and Moose:

Elk, foxes, and coyotes are frequently seen on the upland slopes. Moose are generally seen in the willow areas. Because of the dense forest cover and the high willows, all these animals can be well hidden until they emerge from cover. Always be prepared with your camera on the adjacent seat with your exposure preset.

Site Specific Photography Tips

Bear Photography Tips: Lenses in the 400 to 600mm range are best for bear photography. Keep your camera ready on the passenger seat as you travel Two Ocean Road for grab shots. Many times, the forest edge approaches the roadside, so be very careful when exiting your vehicle due to the limited visibility. If a bear is sniffing the air, be very cautious as there might be another bear approaching the area.

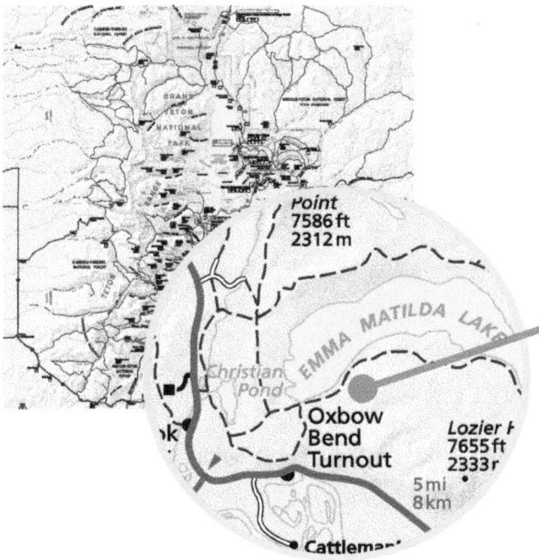

HOTSPOT #27

Oxbow Bend

HIGHLIGHTS:

Oxbow Bend is prime landscape photography location. Reflections off the water surface with Mount Moran and the Tetons in the background make for a memorable image. The area will leave you speechless in the autumn when the cottonwoods, aspen, and willows all change to a beautiful yellow color. Grizzly bears are relatively common near the water's edge and in the surrounding meadows. Eagles are common in the early spring as the ice melts. Waterfowl, such as white pelicans and ducks, are also common from spring through autumn.

DIRECTIONS

Mileage from Jackson Town Square

Travel north on Highway 89 for 30.8 miles. At Moran Junction, turn left and continue on Highway 89 to Oxbow Bend (33.6 miles).

WILDLIFE IN AREA:

Grizzly and Black Bears:

One of Thomas Mangelsen's famous images was made at Oxbow Bend; it includes a grizzly bear and cub crossing the meadow with Mount Moran in the background. Bears are relatively common in the area from April to mid-June and a bit less common September-October.

Birds:

Eagles forage for fish and carcasses in the early spring as the lake ice melts. The white pelicans migrate back to the area in early May. As one of the largest water birds, white pelicans are very majestic. Multiple species of ducks visit the lake area.

Site Specific Photography Tips

Bears: Lenses in the 500 to 600mm range are best to give a sufficient safety margin for the bears and yourself. Images are possible from the car window as the bears cross from the lake side to the hillside.

Birds: Flight shots of eagles and white pelicans are best in morning and evening as midday light can cause harsh shadows. Lenses in the 200 to 600mm range are best for flight shots. At times, eagles sit on the ice surface providing beautiful photo opportunities.

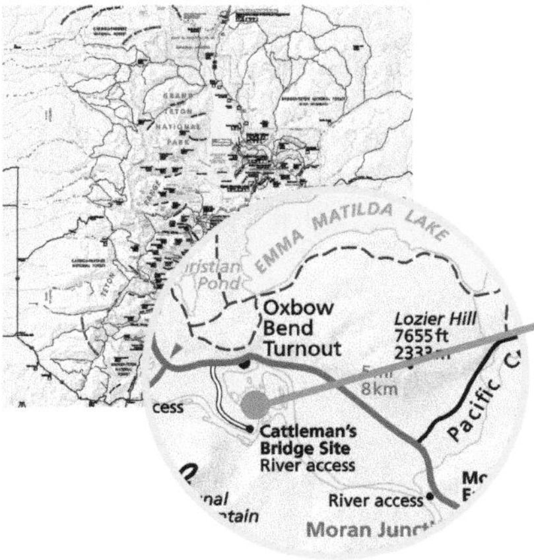

HOTSPOT #28

Cattleman's Landing

HIGHLIGHTS:

Cattleman's Landing is where rancher's cattle would cross the Snake River before there were bridges and cattle transport trailers. It is a scenic drive behind Oxbow Lake and along the Snake River. Elk and moose are common in the area. Mule deer are seen occasionally near the Snake River and waterfowl are common at Oxbow Lake. A beautiful landscape photography location is also located along this stretch, wildflowers are common in the area in late spring, and Mount Moran and the Tetons are directly to the west.

DIRECTIONS

Mileage from Jackson Town Square

Travel north on Highway 89 for 30.8 miles. At Moran Junction, turn left and continue on Highway 89 past Oxbow Bend (33.6 miles), Cattleman's Road is 0.6 miles past Oxbow Bend parking area. The road winds behind Oxbow Lake to the Snake River (0.8 miles).

WILDLIFE IN AREA:

Waterfowl:

White pelicans and ducks are common near Oxbow Lake. This area is good for late afternoon flight shots as the sun will be at your back and the lake to the east. The approach to the lakeside is relatively flat making good images possible from near the water surface.

Elk and Moose:

Elk are most common in the area in late spring and early autumn (April-May and Sept-October). Moose are found near the river and the lake from May through October. Most any area with a concentration of willow will attract moose.

Site Specific Photography Tips

Elk and Moose: Mornings and late afternoon are the best time for photographing elk and moose. Lenses in the 400 to 600mm range will provide frame-filling images and lenses from wide to moderate telephoto will be useful to include the animal with habitat, such as Mount Moran to the west.

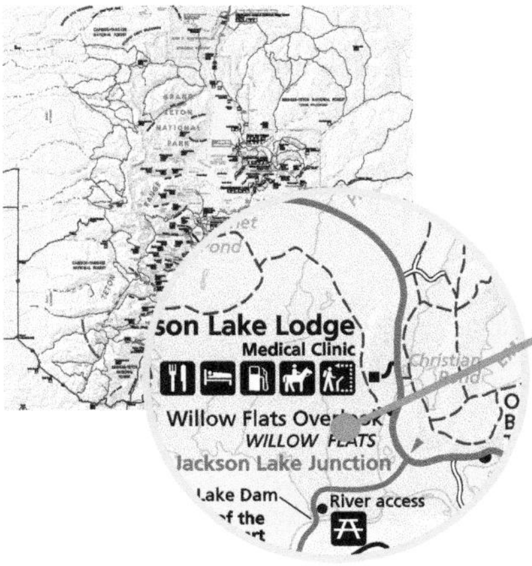

HOTSPOT #29

Willow Flats

HIGHLIGHTS:

Grizzly bears, elk, moose, and sandhill cranes are common in the Willow Flats area. Bears are most common from April-June in the flats whereas sandhill cranes, elk, and moose are common in the flats from May through late September.

DIRECTIONS

Mileage from Jackson Town Square

Travel north on Highway 89 to Moran Junction, turn left and continue on Highway 89 past Oxbow Bend to Willow Flats (34.8 miles).

WILDLIFE IN AREA:

Elk and Moose:

Although elk and moose are relatively common in the flats, they are frequently hidden by the tall willows. On occasion, elk and moose will be in the clearings or up near the large picture windows of Jackson Lake Lodge. During the latter part of May and early June, elk calving occurs in the flats which increases the density of bears.

Grizzly Bears:

Grizzly bears are initially attracted to the flats in April as they forage for rodents and green plants. As elk move into the flats to give birth in May, bears are commonly seen in the flats pursuing this new food source.

MAP 5

Site Specific Photography Tips

Elk and Moose: A patient photographer will have good luck with elk and moose in the flats in the mornings and evenings. Both animals are most active at those times and the golden light of dawn and dusk is pleasing on their dark coats.

Grizzly Bear: Lenses in the 500 to 600mm range are best for bears. You can also shoot from your vehicle window using beanbags and window supports. Watch the sun angle because the area to stand is to the south of the flats with the sun rising to the east and setting to the west. Harsh shadows can be diminished by carefully watching the angle of the bear and sun angle to your camera position. Exercise a modicum of caution around the flats as the bears can be hidden by the willows. For the protection of the bears and yourself, stay near your vehicle and carry bear spray on your person (it does little good in the vehicle or in your backpack).

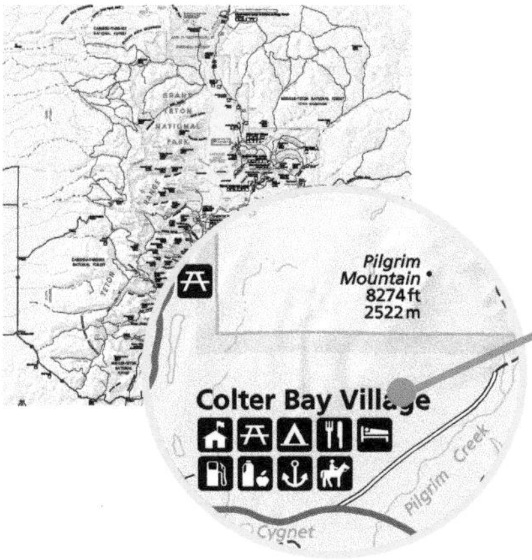

HOTSPOT #30

Pilgrim Creek Road

MAP 5

HIGHLIGHTS:

Pilgrim Creek Road is a wildlife-rich area for grizzly bears, coyotes, elk, and marmots. Grizzlies are seen near the intersection of Pilgrim Creek and Highway 89 in the open meadows and in the Pilgrim Creek Road meadows from late April-June and from August-October. Watch the meadows for coyotes. On occasion, elk are observed near the tree line. Marmots are common at the second concrete block structure (pump house) on the north side of the road (1.8 miles from Highway 89). Bears also frequent the riverbed area at the end of Pilgrim Creek Road.

DIRECTIONS

Mileage from Jackson Town Square

Travel north on Highway 89 to Moran Junction, turn left and continue on Highway 89 to Pilgrim Creek Road (38.5 miles). Pilgrim Creek Road is 2.2 miles long and dead ends at Pilgrim Creek.

WILDLIFE IN AREA:

Grizzly Bears:

Typically, the best way to find grizzly bears is to watch for the "bear jam" of vehicles by the side of the road. When the bears emerge from hibernation in late April to May, they feed on dandelions, rodents (such as ground squirrels), and winter carcasses. As omnivores, they have a diverse diet that includes a wide range of vegetative matter and meat. Grizzly bears have a territory that is roughly eighty-five square miles. They will move around within this area in search of food. Bear #399, the most famous bear in Grand Teton National Park, has a territory that covers from north of Pilgrim Creek south to Elk Ranch and west to Signal Mountain area. It is not unusual to see photographers, during bear season, waiting in their vehicles from sunrise to sunset for bears to appear.

Coyotes:

Coyotes frequent the meadows of Pilgrim Creek Road hunting ground squirrels and other rodents. Patient photographers can get good images of the coyotes hunting in the sagebrush.

Elk:

Elk are seen infrequently near the tree line along Pilgrim Creek Road. Frame-filling images of elk are typically difficult along this stretch. However, photographs showing the habitat with an elk are pleasing.

Marmots:

Turn onto Pilgrim Creek Road and proceed to the second concrete block structure (pump house) (1.8 miles from Highway 89). There is an access road that loops back to the pump house. Walk along the access road. Yellow-bellied marmots are found on the rocks adjacent to the shallow ditch and behind the concrete building. Marmots are also common in the dead trees. Marmots live in burrows or hollow areas of the trees. Marmots hibernate during the winter and emerge in late April. They return to hibernate in late August. Typically, marmots are most active in the sunshine and a bit sluggish in the early mornings and late evenings.

Site Specific Photography Tips

Grizzly Bear: Pilgrim Creek is a prime area for grizzly bears as they feed on tubers, squirrels, and other forage. The meadows are wide open providing numerous opportunities for beautiful images. Wildflowers are in bloom from mid-May through early July. Safety, for yourself and the bears, is the primary concern. Park regulations require you to remain 100 yards from bears and to carry bear spray. Therefore, a 500 to 600mm lens is the best option. Teleconverters are a valuable accessory as they extend your reach.

Marmot: These marmots are excellent photographic subjects as they are accustomed to humans and allow a relatively close approach. Move slow, stay back a bit, and allow the marmot to become accustomed to you. If they duck into their burrows, stand still for a couple minutes and they will usually reappear. Lenses in the 300 to 600mm range are typically best. When the marmots are near their burrows or on the rocks, bed down near the ground for a more pleasing picture.

Coyote: Coyotes are tolerant of humans, especially if you photograph them from the open window of your vehicle. Coyotes can cover a large area hunting for food but the patient photographer can get excellent images. Because there is less traffic on Pilgrim Creek Road, many times you can sit in your vehicle and wait for the coyote to approach the road. Lenses in the 300 to 600mm range are best.

HOTSPOT #31

Dump Road

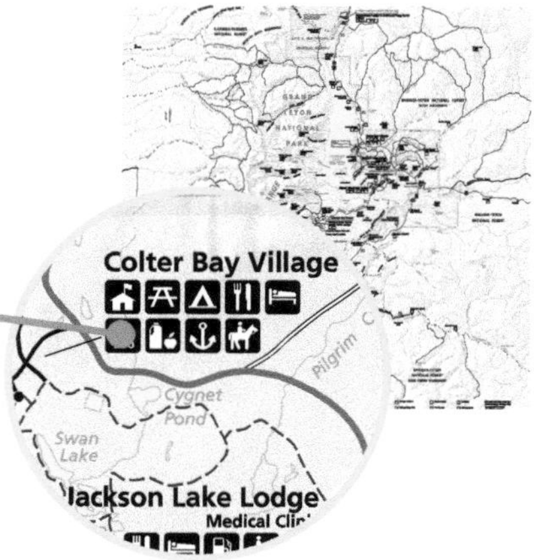

MAP 5

HIGHLIGHTS:

Grizzly bears are the primary attraction for the Dump Road area. The primary hotspot is near the highway although elk, bears, and other animals can be found in the meadows and forests along Dump Road.

DIRECTIONS

Mileage from Jackson Town Square

Travel north on Highway 89 to Moran Junction, turn left and continue on Highway 89 past Pilgrim Creek Road. Dump Road is the next unmarked road to the right (39.7 miles). As you head down Dump Road, the park service maintenance area is to the left (0.3 miles from Highway 89) and the Dump Road continues along the right fork into the forest for a couple miles.

WILDLIFE IN AREA:

Grizzly Bears:

In late April through June and from September through October, bears forage the roadside near the highway. The grassy knoll to the east of Dump Road, along Highway 89, is a popular attraction for bears because of the heavy concentration of flowers and grass. Bears are frequently seen near the highway roadside. On occasion, bears will be seen in forested areas along Dump Road.

Elk:

Elk are occasionally seen along Dump Road from May through October. They emerge from the deep forest canopy at dawn and dusk to feed on grasses and other plants.

MAP 5

Site Specific Photography Tips

Bears and Elk: Bears forage the grassy area adjacent to the forest edge. Lenses in the 200 to 600mm range are best in this area. Because the forest cover is close to the road, it is best to remain inside your vehicle and use a beanbag or other support.

HOTSPOT #32

Colter Bay Junction

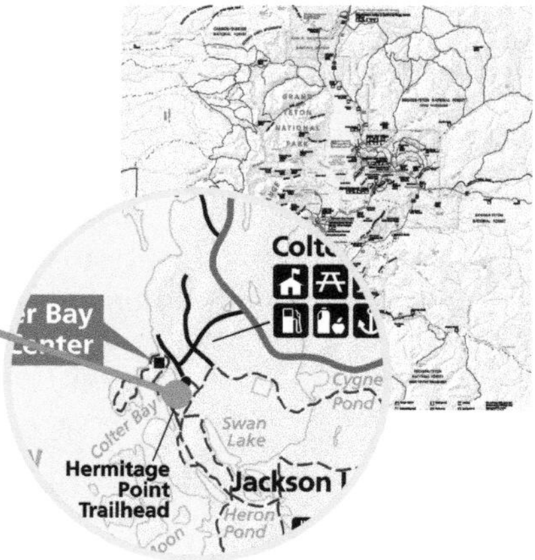

MAP 5

HIGHLIGHTS:

Colter Bay is a campground for tents, RVs, and cabins. Foxes and bears are found in the area. Lake access is available at the boat launch ramp.

DIRECTIONS

Mileage from Jackson Town Square

Travel north on Highway 89 to Moran Junction, turn left and continue on Highway 89 to Colter Bay Junction (34.6 miles).

WILDLIFE IN AREA:

Grizzly and Black Bears:

Grizzly bears are occasionally seen near Swan Lake and near the shoreline of Colter Bay. Anytime you have a concentration of campers with food, bears will be attracted. Make sure to use proper food storage techniques for unused food and food scraps. Bear-proof trashcans are provided for food waste and trash.

Foxes:

Foxes are relatively common in the Colter Bay area, especially along the west end near the visitor's center, to the north of visitor's center, and near the boat launch. From late April through October, foxes are in the forested and meadow areas. In winter, foxes are commonly found near the shoreline, especially near the ice fishing cabins. Although it is against park regulations to feed animals, foxes "steal" fish frequently from the ice fishermen.

Site Specific Photography Tips

Foxes: When the lake is frozen, nice images of foxes crossing the lake are possible. From spring through autumn, images of foxes in the meadows are sure to please. Lenses in the 200 to 600mm range are best for fox images; at times they can be photographed directly from the car window.

Bears: Bears cross through the Colter Bay area frequently and can emerge quickly from the roadside brush. Carry bear spray and exercise extreme caution. Park regulations require you to remain 100 yards from bears and wolves. There are few open areas in the Colter Bay area so it is best to photograph bears from the safety of your vehicle. Use lenses in the 400 to 600mm range for best results.

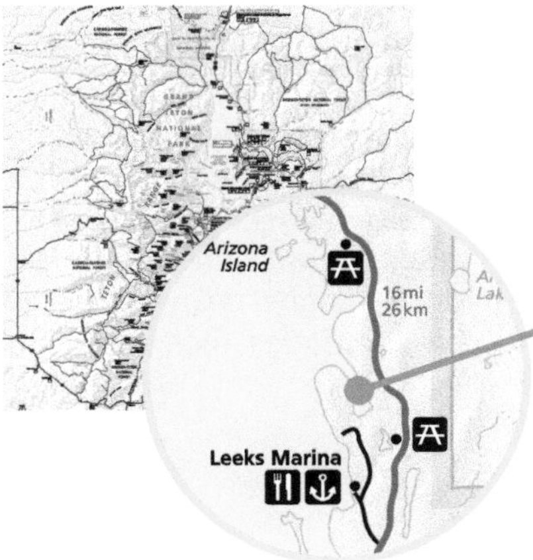

HOTSPOT #33

Highway 89 North of Colter Bay

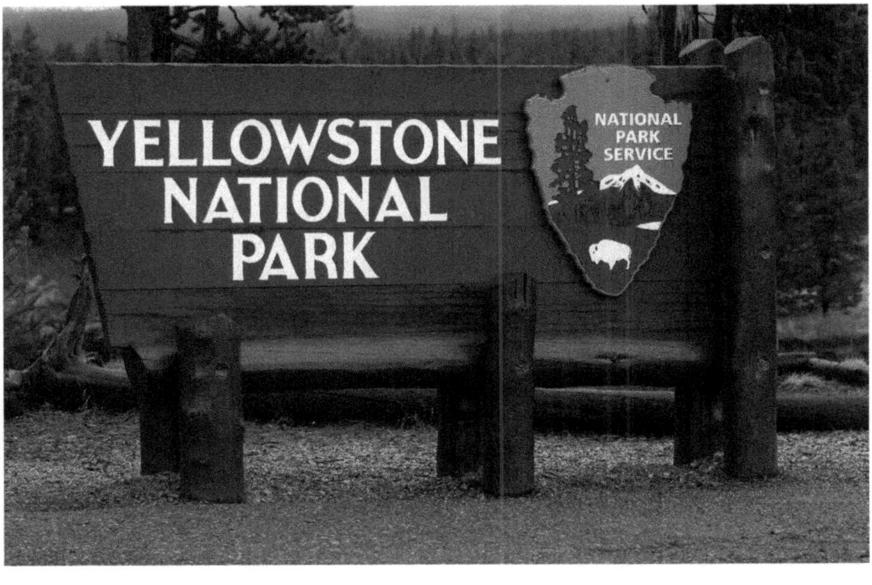

MAP 5

HIGHLIGHTS:

The sixteen miles stretch from Colter Bay Junction to Yellowstone transverses diverse habitats ranging from closed canopy conifer forest to open habitat willow wetland meadows. Most wildlife will be seen near the roadside or in the picnic areas. Wildlife is concentrated in this area because of the proximity to the river, the upland closed canopy forest, and the availability of food. Foxes, skunks, pine martens, elk, moose, and grizzly bears are seen along this stretch. The area north of Colter Bay is not plowed after the heavy snowfall begins. However, in early spring, park service will begin plowing the road which increases the wildlife concentration along the roadside.

DIRECTIONS

Mileage from Jackson Town Square

Travel north on Highway 89 to Moran Junction, turn left and continue on Highway 89 to Colter Bay Junction (34.6 miles). As you continue north, you will pass Leeks Marina and three picnic areas (Sargent Bay, Arizona Island, and Lakeview). Soon past the picnic areas, you will enter the John D. Rockefeller, Jr. Memorial Parkway (43.9 miles) that connects Grand Teton and Yellowstone National Parks. Sheffield Creek and Flagg Ranch are prior to the south entrance to Yellowstone (51 miles).

WILDLIFE IN AREA:

Foxes, Skunks, Elk, and Pine Martens:

Foxes, skunks, and elk tend to be concentrated in the forested areas that include both conifers (evergreens) mixed with aspens and/or cottonwoods. Foxes are found at the picnic areas trying to "steal" scraps of food. Pine martens are most common in the lodgepole pine forest that dominates the area. The smaller animals are difficult to find unless near the roadside. Moose are most common in the willow wetland areas near the riverbeds.

Grizzly Bears:

Grizzly bears are occasionally near the roadside, especially in early spring when the forest canopy is still deep in snow. In addition, bears are seen adjacent to the Snake River just south of the Yellowstone south entrance gate. Exercise extreme care when photographing bears near the roadside to protect the bears and yourself. Lenses in the 400 to 600mm range are necessary for bear images.

Site Specific Photography Tips

Bears: Forest cover extends to the roadside so exercise extreme caution in this area. Always carry bear spray or do photograph from the protection of your vehicle. Lenses in the 400 to 600mm range are best for bears.

Foxes, Skunks, etc: As the snow begins to melt in late April and early May, wildlife will be concentrated near the roadside. During the summer months, occasionally wildlife will be encountered near the roadside areas. Lenses in the 100 to 600 mm range are great for photographing in this area.

COVERING HOTSPOTS #34-40

Map #6

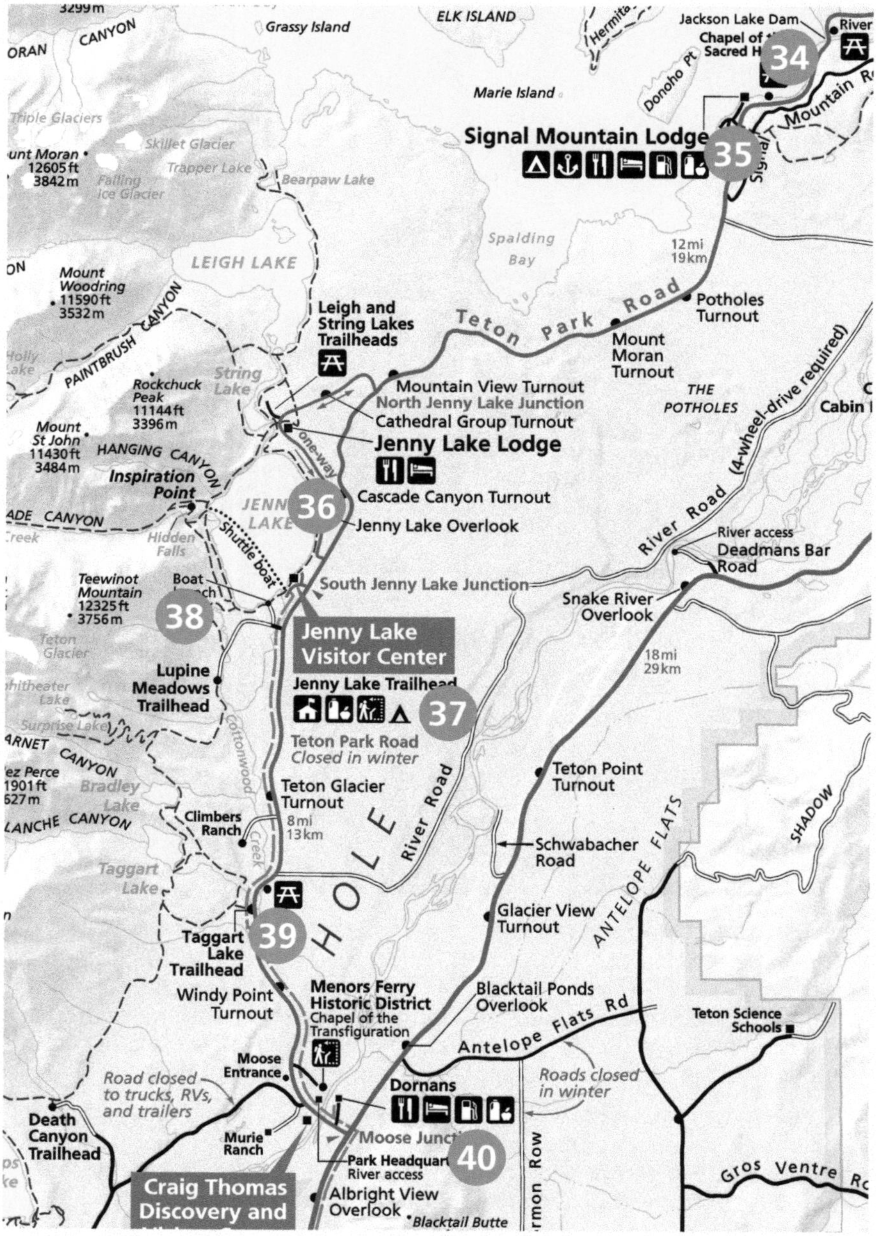
Grassy Island
ELK ISLAND
Hermitage
Jackson Lake Dam
River
Chapel of the Sacred Heart
34
Donoho Pt
Marie Island
Signal Mountain Road
Signal Mountain Lodge
35
CANYON
ORAN
Triple Glaciers
Skillet Glacier
Mount Moran
12605 ft
3842 m
Trapper Lake
Falling Ice Glacier
Bearpaw Lake
Spalding Bay
12 mi
19 km
LEIGH LAKE
Mount Woodring
11590 ft
3532 m
PAINTBRUSH CANYON
Holly Lake
Leigh and String Lakes Trailheads
Teton Park Road
Potholes Turnout
Mount Moran Turnout
THE POTHOLES
River Road (4-wheel-drive required)
Cabin
String Lake
Rockchuck Peak
11144 ft
3396 m
Mountain View Turnout
North Jenny Lake Junction
Cathedral Group Turnout
Mount St John
11430 ft
3484 m
HANGING CANYON
Jenny Lake Lodge
one-way
Inspiration Point
CASCADE CANYON
Creek
JENNY LAKE
36
Cascade Canyon Turnout
Jenny Lake Overlook
Hidden Falls
Shuttle boat
River access
Deadmans Bar Road
Teewinot Mountain
12325 ft
3756 m
Boat Launch
South Jenny Lake Junction
Snake River Overlook
38
Teton Glacier
Jenny Lake Visitor Center
18 mi
29 km
Lupine Meadows Trailhead
Amphitheater Lake
Jenny Lake Trailhead
37
Surprise Lake
GARNET CANYON
Teton Park Road
Closed in winter
Nez Perce
11901 ft
3627 m
Bradley Lake
Cottonwood Creek
Teton Point Turnout
Teton Glacier Turnout
River Road
AVALANCHE CANYON
Climbers Ranch
8 mi
13 km
Schwabacher Road
ANTELOPE FLATS
SHADOW
Taggart Lake
JACKSON HOLE
Glacier View Turnout
Taggart Lake Trailhead
39
Windy Point Turnout
Menors Ferry Historic District
Chapel of the Transfiguration
Blacktail Ponds Overlook
Antelope Flats Rd
Teton Science Schools
Moose Entrance
Road closed to trucks, RVs, and trailers
Dornans
Roads closed in winter
Death Canyon Trailhead
Murie Ranch
Moose Junction
Park Headquarters
River access
40
Mormon Row
Gros Ventre Road
Craig Thomas Discovery and Visitor Center
Albright View Overlook
Blacktail Butte

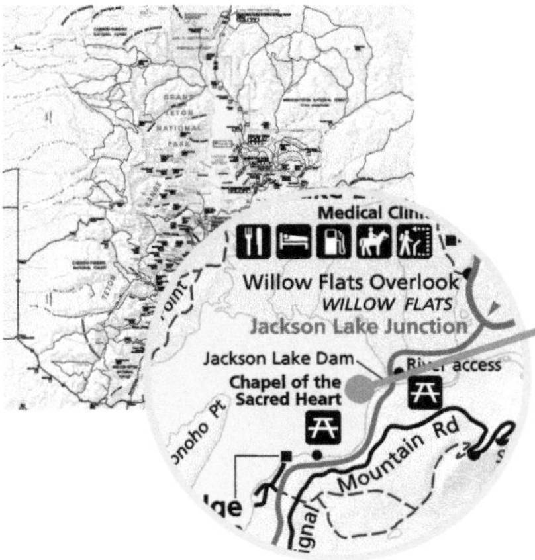

HOTSPOT #34

Jackson Lake Dam

MAP 6

HIGHLIGHTS:

Moose are common in the wetland area and boat launch parking area. Grizzly and black bears occur in the area as they search for fish along the shoreline and cross from Willow Flats to Oxbow Bend. When the ice begins to melt on Jackson Lake, otters feed on fish near the shoreline. White pelicans occasionally forage the water near the dam weir.

DIRECTIONS

Mileage from Jackson Town Square

Travel north on Highway 89 to Moran Junction, turn left and continue on Highway 89 past Oxbow Bend to Jackson Lake Junction. Turn left and proceed to Jackson Lake Dam (36.2 miles). Alternately, travel up the inside loop, Teton Park Road from Moose Junction to the dam (19.9 miles from Moose Junction).

WILDLIFE IN AREA:

Moose:

Moose feed among the willows in the wetland area adjacent to the boat launch road (wormhole area). Many times, moose are standing in the water as they feed on the willows.

Bears and Otters:

Bears and otters are attracted to the shoreline as the winter ice begins to recede because fish are concentrated in this area. From late April through June, bears patrol the dam area and wormhole as they cross from Willow Flats to Oxbow Bend.

White Pelicans:

The pelicans venture south for winter but return to the area in May and stay until September. Unlike brown pelicans, white pelicans do not dive from the air into the water for fish; they feed more like ducks bobbing underwater for food.

MAP 6

Site Specific Photography Tips

Moose: Frequently, the numerous willow twigs in the area can obstruct moose but they typically move about frequently providing opportunities for clear images. Moose strip leaves from the willows that is an interesting photo as the willow twig is pulled through the mouth (see image at Hotspot 44).

Bears: When the bears are near the shoreline, it is best to get images from the roadside. The roadside is elevated from the shoreline but far enough away to provide a measure of protection. When the bears finish foraging for fish, they will typically cross the road to the wormhole and willow area heading toward Oxbow Bend. Lenses in the 400 to 600mm range are best for bear photography.

Otters: Many times, otters will catch a fish in the water and come out onto the ice to eat their prey. If you move carefully and slowly, you can approach the otters close enough for nice images using a 300 to 600mm lenses from near the shoreline.

Pelicans: The Snake River exits the dam heading east. Flight shots from the roadway atop the dam provide nice lighting in the late afternoon and early evening. Pelicans floating on the water surface are best near dawn and dusk because of the softer lighting. Because these birds are nearly all white, watch your exposure carefully; it is easy to overexpose the whites thereby losing all detail.

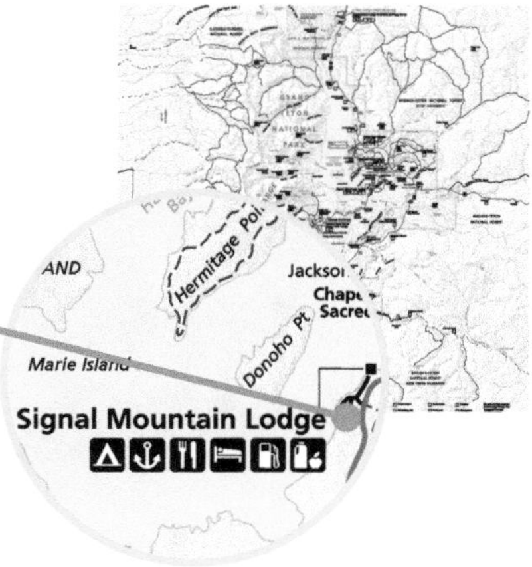

HOTSPOT #35

Signal Mountain and Signal Mountain Lodge area

MAP 6

HIGHLIGHTS:

The summit road and the camping areas are open from May through October however closed to vehicle traffic once the snow begins to accumulate in winter. Take a trip to the summit for a wide expansive view of Jackson Hole valley and the winding Snake River. Signal Mountain and the lodge area is a hotspot for black bears and occasionally grizzly bears. Mule deer and foxes are frequently seen in the forested areas and along the roadside. Foxes occasionally will be near the boat launch ramp and camping areas of Signal Mt. Lodge seeking free food. Blue grouse are seen in the forested areas along the road to the summit.

DIRECTIONS

Mileage from Jackson Town Square

Travel north on Highway 89 to Moose Junction (12.6 miles). Turn left (west) and along Teton Park Road to the Signal Mountain (29.7 miles) and Signal Mountain lodge area (30.8 miles).

WILDLIFE IN AREA:

Bears:

Black bears hibernate from late October through April. Once they appear from hibernation, they are occasionally seen along the road to the summit of Signal Mountain and crossing to Signal Mountain Lodge area. In May and early June, dandelions growing near the roadside and open meadows are their major food source. The camping area near the lodge attracts the bears as they come looking for a free meal. On rare occasions, grizzlies also cross through this area.

Mule Deer:

Mule deer are common in the forested areas leading toward the boat launch and camping areas. They are also common along Teton Park Road between the lodge and the summit road. Deer forage for grasses and occasionally leaves of shrubs. If you pull your car onto the shoulder of the road but do not exit the car, deer will usually continue to eat their meals without fleeing the area.

Blue Grouse:

On rare occasions, blue grouse are seen along the summit road in the forested areas. Grouse are about the size of a small chicken. They will typically not fly unless disturbed, preferring to run off to cover.

MAP 6

Site Specific Photography Tips

Bears: Most bear images in this area will be captured from the vehicle window. With exposure preset and camera on the seat adjacent to the driver, obtaining a quick image will be a straightforward process.

Deer: Obtaining images from the vehicle window is easy using lenses in the 100 to 400mm range. On occasion, you will be able to exit the car and approach slowly for additional images.

HOTSPOT #36

Jenny Lake and Cascade Canyon

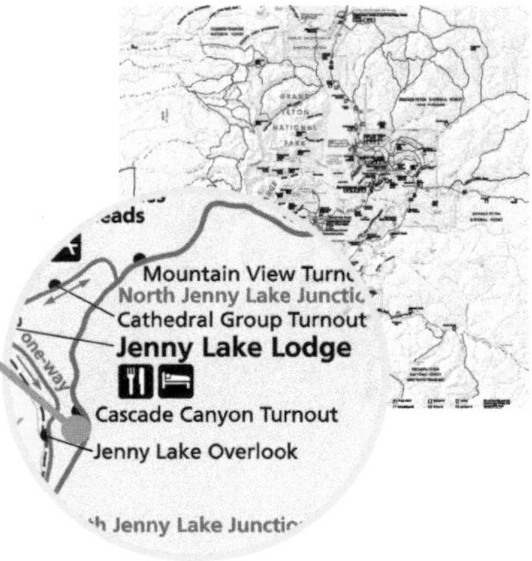

MAP 6

HIGHLIGHTS:

The Jenny Lake area is a popular area for hikers, wildlife enthusiasts, and landscape photographers. The north entrance accesses String Lake, Jenny Lake Lodge, and Jenny Lake overlook. The south entrance accesses the boat launch and trailhead to Cascade Canyon and the Jenny Lake loop. Cascade Canyon is a relatively gentle climb in elevation through forested habitat with moose, black bears, and pika.

DIRECTIONS

Mileage from Jackson Town Square

Travel north on Highway 89 past Gros Ventre Junction to Moose Junction. Turn left (west) and proceed through the entry gate. Travel up the inside loop from Moose Junction to the Jenny Lake parking lot (7.8 miles).

WILDLIFE IN AREA:

Moose:

Moose are common along the west side of Jenny Lake and along the trail up toward Cascade Canyon. Moose Pond, roughly 2.4 miles from the trailhead near the Jenny Lake visitor's center, is a popular spot to see moose. Moose feed on the willows, cottonwoods, and aspens. When they are bedded down, they can almost disappear in the brush so be careful hiking, as a startled moose can be a dangerous moose.

Pika:

As you hike up in elevation to the more exposed rocky areas, you will encounter pika living in the rock crevices. Pika are related to rabbits and are about the size of ground squirrels, though they are tail-less. They typically scurry around eating grass and collecting "hay" for their dens.

MAP 6

Bears:

As you hike up Cascade Canyon, black bears are not uncommon. Carry bear spray on your belt and hike in groups for protection. Many city folks will tell you that the best bear sighting is the "south end of a northbound bear" fleeing into the forest. In dense forest, that is usually a good sighting but with careful observation, many times you can sight the bear well ahead of your travels. Watching a bear from a safe distance will be a joyous memory you take back home and relive multiple times.

MAP 6

Site Specific Photography Tips

Moose: Arguably, moose are one of the most photogenic of the animals with a variety of facial expressions, big ears, and long legs attached to a massive body. When feeding, moose will move about providing plenty of opportunities for a variety of images. Lenses in the 100 to 400mm range are small enough to carry on a hike but long enough to provide nice images from a safe distance. Exercise caution with moose by staying at least 25 yards away.

Bears: Because black bears are dark, they can be difficult to photograph under the forest canopy. Many times, one must be satisfied with a "record shot" but with patience, bears will move to more open areas of the forest or an open trail. Hiking with a 600mm lens and tripod is not easy but using a handheld crop-sensor body with a zoom lens in the 100 to 400mm range will provide enough reach for good images.

Pika: Pika will perch on rocks watching for predators. Beautiful images can be obtained of these little creatures in their natural habitat. Using an aperture of f8 or less will provide a pleasing out of focus background. Using f11 or greater will include some of the rock environment in your image.

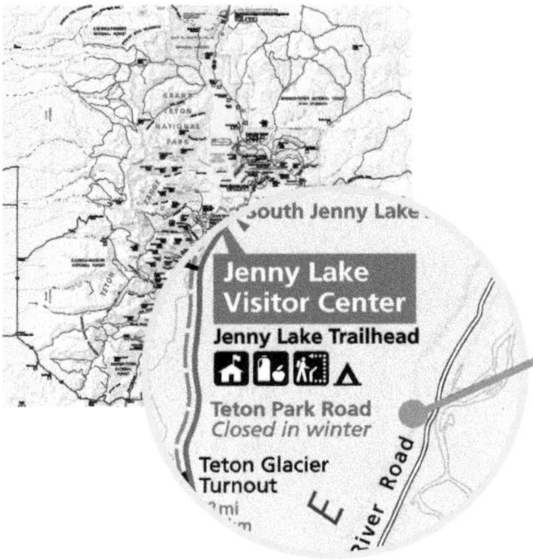

HOTSPOT #37

River Road

HIGHLIGHTS:

If you wish to get away from the crowds and have a bit of solitude, River Road is an excellent drive. However, the road can be very bumpy and rough, at times requiring a four-wheel drive vehicle. Most of the area is open sagebrush meadow. Elk and pronghorn are common in the meadows and mule deer are common near the river.

DIRECTIONS

Mileage from Jackson Town Square

Turn west at Moose Junction and continue to the south entrance of River Road (4.1 miles from Moose Junction). The north entrance to River Road is 0.1 miles south of Signal Mountain Summit entrance. From either the north or the south entrance, River Road heads east roughly 6 miles before turning parallel to the north-south running Snake River.

WILDLIFE IN AREA:

Elk and Mule Deer:

Grasses in the sagebrush meadows attract deer and elk. As the heavy snow melts in early May, animals move back into the open meadows to feed. Elk and deer are most common at dawn and dusk. During the elk the rut (September), bull elk are bugling in the meadows with their harem of cow elk.

Pronghorn:

Unlike most four-legged herbivores, pronghorn are active and graze in the middle of the day. As North America's fastest land mammal, they use their excellent eyesight and amazing speed to escape predators. Typically, pronghorn are in the open meadows because that is where their speed is of the best advantage.

Site Specific Photography Tips

Elk, Deer, and Pronghorn: Because River Road is traveled much less than other roads, the animals are a bit less skittish and more tolerant of vehicles and humans. The sagebrush will provide a pleasing background for these animals. Use lenses in the 400 to 600mm range.

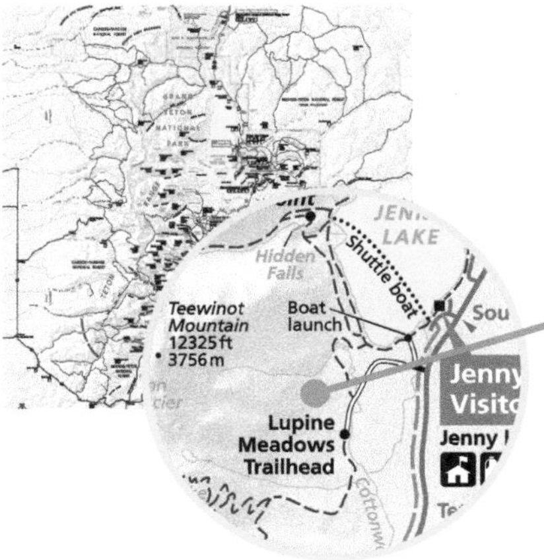

HOTSPOT #38

Lupine Meadows

HIGHLIGHTS:

Lupine Meadows is the trailhead for Grand Teton, Middle and South Teton, Disappointment Peak, Nez Perce, Mount Owen, Teewinot, and Cloudveil Dome. Moose, elk, deer, pika, and black bears are common along this trail to the peaks. Elk are also common in Lupine Meadows near the trailhead area. Bears can be spotted on the slopes of the peaks from the parking area using binoculars and spotting scopes. Broken Falls, one of the tallest cascades in the Tetons, is visible and audible from the Lupine Meadows trailhead parking area. Broken Falls runs heavy with snowmelt from May into July.

DIRECTIONS

Mileage from Jackson Town Square

Travel north on Highway 89 past Gros Ventre Junction to Moose Junction. Turn left (west) and proceed through the entry gate. Travel up the inside loop from Moose Junction to the Lupine Meadows (19.9 miles). Turn left at Lupine Meadows Junction and follow the road over the bridge. Follow the fork southwest toward Lupine Meadows. The trailhead parking area is 1.5 miles from the junction.

WILDLIFE IN AREA:

Elk:

Elk are present in the meadows from May through October. In fact, during the heat of the summer, Lupine Meadows is the one place in the park you can almost guarantee finding elk in the mornings and evenings. From the parking area, look toward the forested area to the southeast with binoculars or spotting scopes.

Black Bears:

The number one animal that tourists wish to see are bears. Because they head into the high country when summer heat intensifies, they can be difficult to locate during peak tourist season. From the parking areas, use binoculars or spotting scopes to scan the mountain slopes of Teewinot, Grand Teton, and Mount Owen for black bears. Bears are frequently active in the mornings and late afternoon. It may take a few minutes, but you can typically find bears on the mountainsides from this location.

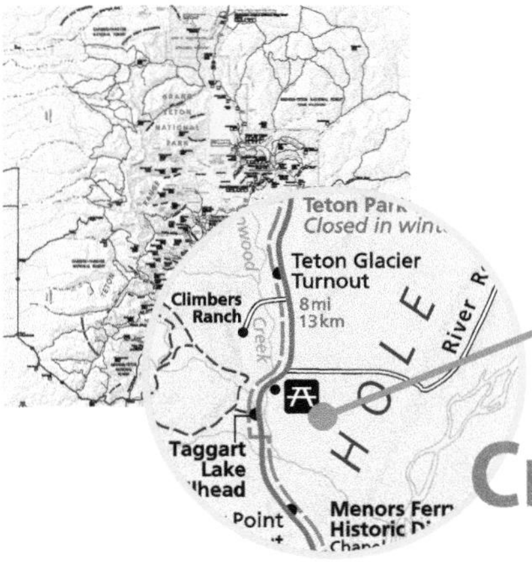

HOTSPOT #40

Cottonwood Creek picnic area

MAP 6

HIGHLIGHTS:

Foxes are frequently seen in the Cottonwood picnic area and beavers are seen in the Cottonwood Creek area. Occasionally, elk are seen in the meadow of the J. Manges Cabin area across Teton Park Road. Manges Cabin is also an excellent landscape photography location.

DIRECTIONS

Mileage from Jackson Town Square

Travel north on Highway 89 turning left at Moose Junction. The Cottonwood picnic area is just a few miles past the entrance gate.

WILDLIFE IN AREA:

Beavers:

Beavers are found in the Cottonwood Creek area, typically building and maintaining dams. Beavers are most active at dawn and dusk.

Foxes:

Although it is against park regulations to feed animals, foxes are frequent visitors to the picnic area. They also hunt the Cottonwood Creek picnic area.

MAP 6

Site Specific Photography Tips

Foxes: Lenses in the 100-400mm range work well when the foxes come near the tables. Remember not to feed the wildlife as a "fed animal is a dead animal." The park service will remove animals that become a nuisance.

Beavers: Because of wet fur, beavers are difficult subjects to photograph well but early morning and late afternoon light are complimentary. Beavers can be skittish, so lenses in the 400-600mm range give sufficient reach.

Map #7

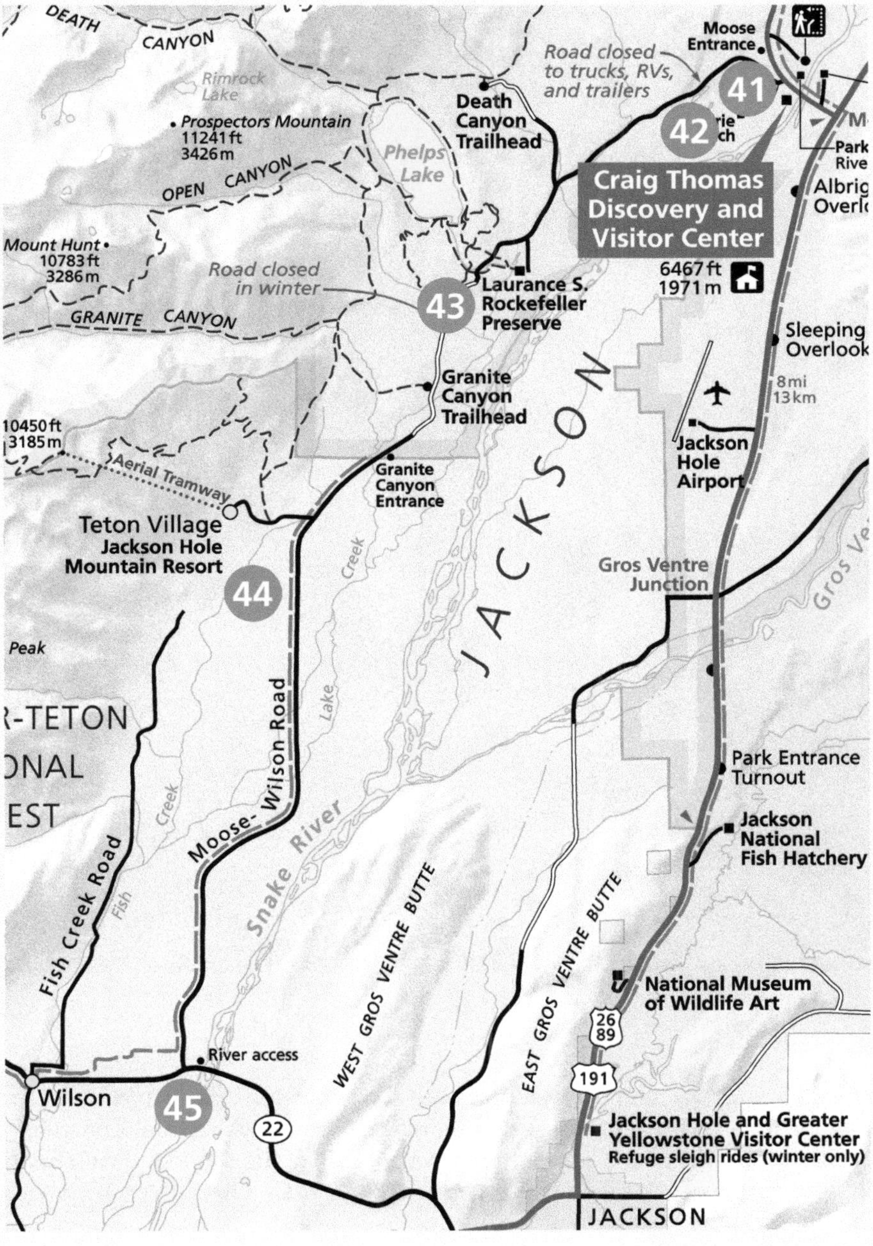
DEATH
CANYON
Rimrock Lake
Prospectors Mountain
11241 ft
3426 m
Phelps Lake
Death Canyon Trailhead
Road closed to trucks, RVs, and trailers
Moose Entrance
41
42
OPEN CANYON
Craig Thomas Discovery and Visitor Center
Mount Hunt
10783 ft
3286 m
Road closed in winter
43
Laurance S. Rockefeller Preserve
6467 ft
1971 m
GRANITE CANYON
Sleeping Overlook
Granite Canyon Trailhead
8 mi
13 km
10450 ft
3185 m
Aerial Tramway
Granite Canyon Entrance
Jackson Hole Airport
Teton Village
Jackson Hole Mountain Resort
JACKSON
44
Gros Ventre Junction
Peak
Creek
Lake
Park Entrance Turnout
Moose-Wilson Road
Snake River
Jackson National Fish Hatchery
Fish Creek Road
Fish
WEST GROS VENTRE BUTTE
EAST GROS VENTRE BUTTE
National Museum of Wildlife Art
26
89
191
River access
Wilson
45
22
Jackson Hole and Greater Yellowstone Visitor Center
Refuge sleigh rides (winter only)
JACKSON

HOTSPOT #41

Moose-Wilson Road, north end to overlook

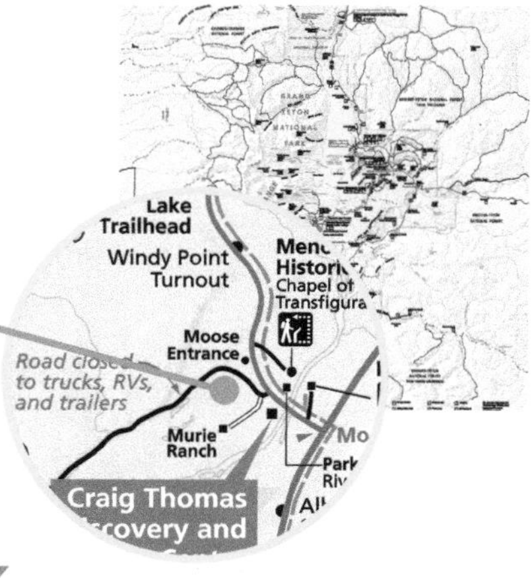

MAP 7

HIGHLIGHTS:

Moose frequently feed on aquatic plants at the overlook pond and are seen bedded down adjacent to the pond shoreline. Great gray owls are seen in the cottonwood trees to the west of the road and north of the overlook. Foxes hunt in the meadows to the west of the roadside. Black bears are relatively common in August on the trail south of the overlook.

DIRECTIONS

Mileage from Jackson Town Square

Travel north on Highway 89 past Gros Ventre Junction; turn left at Moose Junction. Travel past Dornan's and the visitor's center to Moose-Wilson Road. Turn left and proceed past Murie Ranch Road, travel around the corner and uphill to the overlook (14.1 miles).

WILDLIFE IN AREA:

Moose:

A couple years ago, it was possible to photograph moose from the shoreline while they fed on aquatic plants but signs now restrict people to the upper areas. Lenses in the 300-600mm range will provide nice frame filling images of the moose bedded down near the pond.

Foxes:

Foxes are relatively common in the meadows once snow accumulates (November through March) and a bit less common during the summer season. At times, foxes are approachable but lenses in the 300-600mm range are best, either from the vehicle window, tripod mounted, or handheld.

Black Bears:

Chokecherry and hawthorn shrubs are common along the path south of the overlook. Berries on these plants ripen in mid-August attracting black bears. Frequently, bears will work a shrub until all ripe berries are consumed. However, many times berries ripen sequentially which will have the bears returning to the area over a multiple week periods until all berries are consumed.

Site Specific Photography Tips

Black Bears: Photographing black bears under a canopy of trees can be difficult as a dark bear with limited light results in a less than pleasing images. Frequently, bears will work a shrub until all ripe berries are consumed. The bears move around and a patient photographer will get multiple opportunities to photograph bears in the light. Be cautious of bears with cubs as they frequently become separated from their mothers. Sows are protective of their cubs.

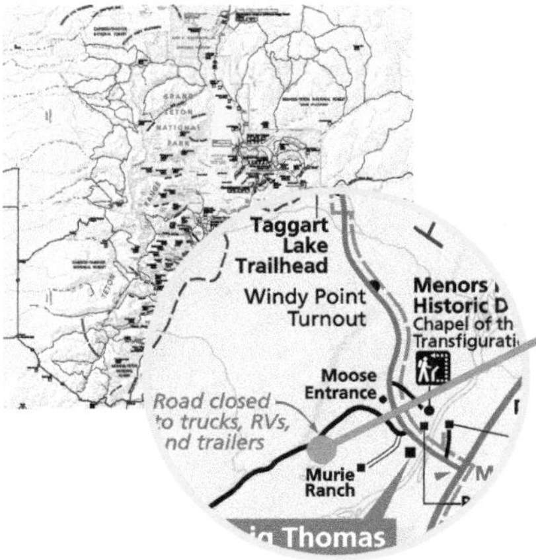

Moose-Wilson Road, sawmill and beaver ponds

HIGHLIGHTS:

Beavers have constructed numerous dams that have slowed the water flow and provided numerous ponds in the area. Moose forage this area for willow and aquatic plants. Chokecherry and hawthorn bushes are common near the roadside. These bushes have berries that ripen in August attracting black bears.

DIRECTIONS

Mileage from Jackson Town Square

Travel north on Highway 89 past Gros Ventre Junction; turn left at Moose Junction. Travel past Dornan's and the visitor's center to Moose-Wilson Road. Turn left and proceed past Murie Ranch Road, travel around the corner and uphill to the overlook. Continue south past the sawmill ponds (15.0 miles) to the beaver pond (15.1 miles).

WILDLIFE IN AREA:

Moose:

The roadside is near the same elevation as the wetland area. On occasion, it is possible to create nice images of moose eating aquatic plants. Moose also eat the willow shrubs near the roadside and to the east of the ponds.

Black Bears:

The abundant ripe berries on the chokecherry and hawthorn shrubs attract black bears. These berries ripen in August. Many times, the bears will climb into the shrubs to obtain the berries providing sufficient time for nice images.

Beavers:

Beavers are generally active at dawn and dusk, which is also the best time to photograph them with the golden light. The golden light reflects off the water surface providing a nice contrast to the dark animals.

Site Specific Photography Tips

Moose: Moose will stand in the water, dip their heads under the water surface, and raise their heads to eat the aquatic plants. When they raise their heads, streams of water will drip from their head. Lenses in the 400-600mm range are best to provide a safe distance from the moose. A shutter speed of 1/125 sec or greater will freeze the water as it drips from the moose's nose. Late afternoon or early evening usually provides the best lighting on blue-sky days because the roadside is to the west of the wetland. However, on heavy overcast days, the light is sufficiently diffused to provide good lighting in the early mornings. At times, you can venture off the roadway to obtain different light angles.

Bears: Many times, leaves and limbs will cover the bear's face as they forage but with a bit of patience, nice clean images are possible. Watch for the bear cubs, as they will be frequently playing in the trees and shrubs. Lenses in the 400-600mm range are best for bear photography.

HOTSPOT #43

Laurance S. Rockefeller (LSR) Preserve and Moose-Wilson south to Teton Village

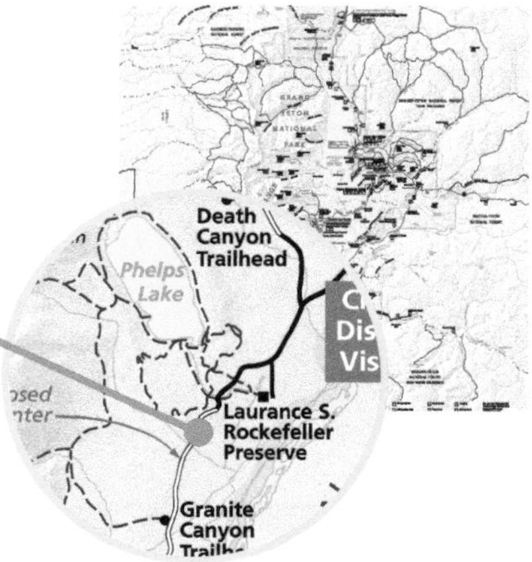

HIGHLIGHTS:

Elk are commonly seen in the meadows south of the LSR Preserve at dawn and dusk from May through October. Great gray owls occasionally hunt the meadows for rodents. Moose and mule deer are encountered in the forested stretches and the river areas along Moose-Wilson Road. Osprey are common south of the Granite Canyon entrance station.

MAP 7

DIRECTIONS

Mileage from Jackson Town Square

Travel north on Highway 89 past Gros Ventre Junction; turn left at Moose Junction. Travel past Dornan's and the visitor's center to Moose-Wilson Road. Turn left and proceed past Murie Ranch Road, travel around the corner and uphill to the overlook. Continue south past the sawmill and beaver ponds to Death Canyon (16.4 miles) to LSR area (16.5 miles). Teton Village is a couple miles south of the Granite Canyon entrance gate.

WILDLIFE IN AREA:

Elk, Deer, and Moose:

Elk are common at dawn and dusk in the meadows to the south and north of Laurance S. Rockefeller (LSR) Preserve. During the rut (late September), the air is alive with the bugling of bulls as they seek their harem of cows. Deer and moose are seen in the forested areas south of LSR. Many times, moose are bedded down (near the roadside) under the trees in summer.

Birds:

On occasion, great gray owls hunt the narrow roadside meadows outside the LSR and the open meadows inside LSR Preserve. Typically, they perch on limbs about 10-15 feet off the ground watching for rodent movements. This section of road is closed to vehicle traffic during winter (November to early May) but open to cross-country skiers and those on snowshoes. An osprey nest is located just south of the Granite Canyon entrance gate atop a single pole adjacent to the road. Osprey return to the park in early May and quickly begin nesting building activity. Osprey will use a nest repeatedly, adding a bit of new material for each season.

Site Specific Photography Tips

Elk, Deer, and Moose: Elk tend to be far from the roadside but environmental images of the animals in the meadows are striking. At dawn, the fog may linger a bit providing a dramatic shot of elk in the meadow. Moose and deer are near the roadside along this stretch so be ready with preset exposures for images from your vehicle window. Moose and deer are tolerant of vehicles. However, if you exit your vehicle, they will flee almost immediately.

HOTSPOT #44

Teton Village to Wyoming 22

(Snake River area of WY 22)

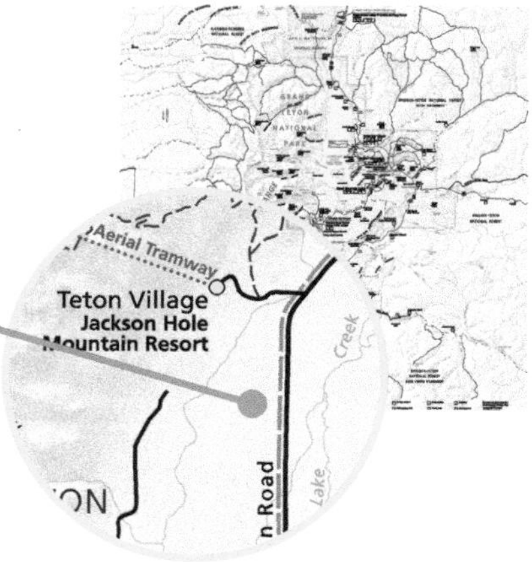

MAP 7

HIGHLIGHTS:

The area from Teton Village to Wyoming 22 bisects residential and ranch areas with wetlands and open meadows. Moose are common in the wetland areas. Elk and foxes are common in the open meadows.

DIRECTIONS

Mileage from Jackson Town Square

From the town square, travel southwest on Broadway to Highway WY 22 and turn right. Continue past the first traffic light (Spring Gulch Road); the road will continue adjacent to ranches and wetland areas. After crossing the Snake River, Teton Village Road is at the next traffic light.

WILDLIFE IN AREA:

Moose:

Fish Creek roughly parallels Moose-Wilson Road that connects Wyoming 22 and Teton Village. This provides a low wetland area with plenty of willows that attracts moose. Moose are frequently near the roadside feeding on willows from May through October. They are common near the Snake River-Rendezvous Park area and the Teton Village. Moose are also relatively common southwest of Teton Mountain Lodge in the willows surrounding the condos on Cody Lane. As snow accumulates in the wetlands (November through April), moose are more concentrated near the roadside and are frequently seen along the bike path adjacent to the roadside.

Elk:

Herds of elk are common in the ranch meadows near the roadside at dawn and dusk from May through November. As snow accumulates, elk move to the National Elk Refuge and other feed grounds.

Fox:

Foxes are common in the parking area of Teton Village in the mornings.

Site Specific Photography Tips

Moose: Moose will frequently feed near the roadside on the willows. Nice images can be obtained from the safety of your vehicle window using lenses in the 100 to 400mm range.

Foxes: Foxes occasionally cross the parking area of Teton Village. A 100 to 400mm lens will be sufficient to get nice images if you are lucky enough to be "in the right place at the right time."

HOTSPOT #45

Wyoming 22 west through Wilson and across Teton Pass

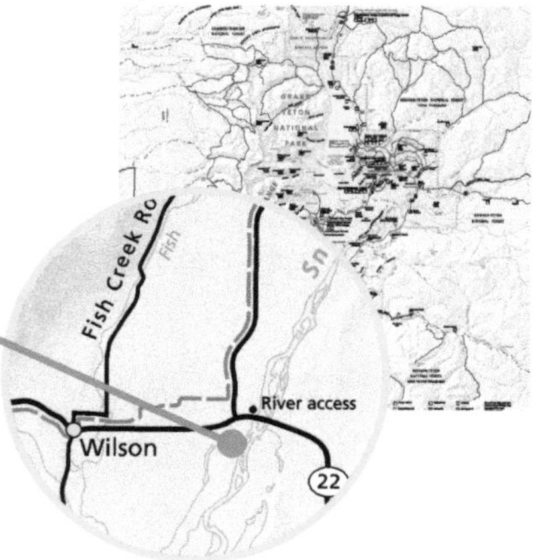

HIGHLIGHTS:

Moose are common in the pond to the south of Wyoming 22 at Moose-Wilson Road. Moose, deer, and elk become more abundant as you approach the town of Wilson. Fish Creek crosses under Wyoming 22 east of the Exxon station. Teton Pass is a steep mountain pass that connects Jackson to Idaho. Moose are also abundant on the Idaho side along the south side of the highway near the ponds.

DIRECTIONS

Mileage from Jackson Town Square

From the town square, travel southwest on Broadway to Highway WY 22, turn right. Continue past the first traffic light (Spring Gulch Road); the road will continue adjacent to ranches and wetland areas. After crossing the Snake River, Teton Village Road is at the next traffic light. Continue on WY 22, past Teton Village Road into the town of Wilson. Teton Pass is soon after the town center.

WILDLIFE IN AREA:

Moose, Deer, and Elk:

Fish Creek in Wilson is a low wetland area with abundant willows. In late May and June, cow elk use this area and the drainage further south into the Snake River as a calving area. Moose and deer are common in the area throughout the year. Moose are also abundant on the Idaho side of the pass in the ponds adjacent to the highway. These ponds are also surrounded by willows, which are a ready food source for the moose and provides cover for protection from predators.

MAP 7

Site Specific Photography Tips

Moose, Deer, and Elk: Many times, these animals will be near the roadside and lenses in the 100 to 400mm range are sufficient to get frame-filling images.

Eagles and other birds: Eagles are occasionally signed on top of the telephone poles, especially near the creeks. Lenses in the 100 to 400mm range provide nice images of the eagles. Many times, smaller birds are on the fence posts. Typically long lenses (500 to 600mm) are needed for these small birds.

Map #8

COVERING HOTSPOTS #46-47

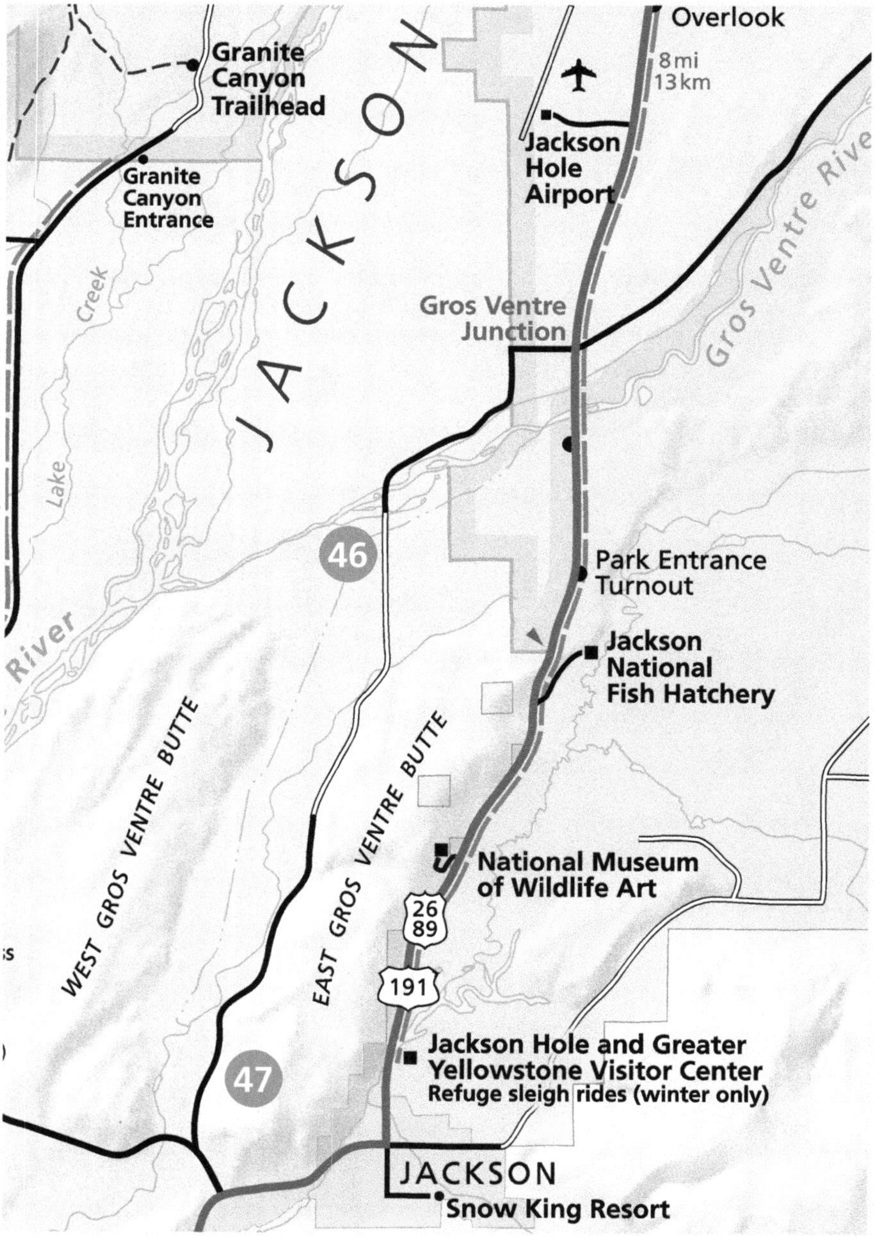

Overlook
8 mi
13 km
Granite
Canyon
Trailhead
Granite
Canyon
Entrance
JACKSON
Jackson
Hole
Airport
Creek
Gros Ventre
Junction
Gros Ventre River
Lake
46
Park Entrance
Turnout
River
Jackson
National
Fish Hatchery
WEST GROS VENTRE BUTTE
EAST GROS VENTRE BUTTE
National Museum
of Wildlife Art
26
89
191
47
Jackson Hole and Greater
Yellowstone Visitor Center
Refuge sleigh rides (winter only)
JACKSON
Snow King Resort

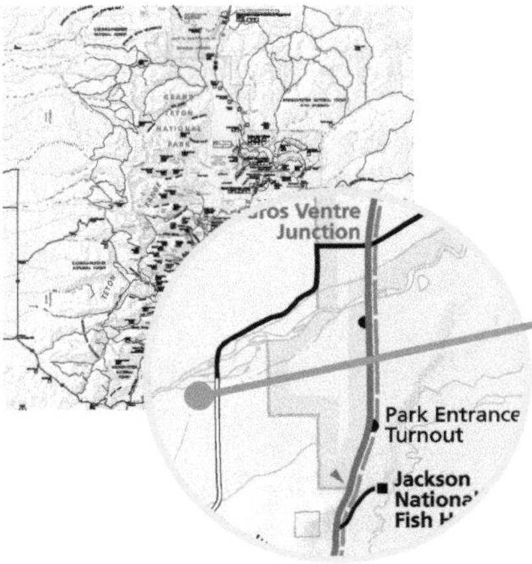

HOTSPOT #46

Spring Gulch Road

HIGHLIGHTS:

Moose, white-tail and mule deer, elk, foxes, marmots, osprey, bald eagles, and owls (great gray and great horned) are frequently encountered in the northern portion of Spring Gulch Road whereas elk and occasionally wolves are encountered on the southern stretch of Spring Gulch Road.

DIRECTIONS

Mileage from Jackson Town Square

From the town square, travel southwest on Broadway to Highway WY 22. Continue to the first traffic light and turn right (Spring Gulch Road).

WILDLIFE IN AREA:

Moose, Elk, and Deer:

Moose are common along the north section of Spring Gulch Road during winter. As snow accumulates, moose will spend increasing amount of time by the roadside foraging on cottonwood, willow, and aspen twigs. Along the northern stretch of the road, elk and deer are numerous in spring (April-May) and fall (September-November) but also encountered near the meadows and forest canopy areas in summer (June-August). Elk are also numerous in the ranch areas along the southern stretch of the road.

Marmots and Foxes:

Marmots are common from May through August on the golf course area. These marmots can be a bit skittish, ducking into burrows as soon as you park your car. However, a patient photographer will be rewarded when they re-emerge from their burrows. Foxes hunt for rodents in the meadows and forested areas. On occasion, they bed down near the base of the Gros Ventre bridge.

Owls, Bald Eagles, and Osprey:

Owls frequent the cottonwood forest canopy nearly year-round. Typically, they will be in an area for a couple months, have an interrupted period, and return to the area again. Eagles and osprey fish and nest near the Gros Ventre River area. Osprey are found nesting on poles with platforms near the golf course and eagles nest in the forested areas in large trees such as cottonwoods.

Site Specific Photography Tips

Moose, Elk, and Deer: Deer commonly forage for grasses by the roadside whereas elk forage the golf course area and the meadows. Lenses in the 100-400mm range work well for images from the vehicle window whereas lenses in the 300-600mm range work better for images of the animals in the meadows. Moose occasionally bed down in the residential areas providing some nice photography opportunities.

Raptors: Occasionally, owls will perch and hunt from trees close to the roadside. Lenses in the 300-600mm range provide frame-filling images. Flight shots are difficult of owls as they do not frequently fly in the open areas. Most flight shots will be cluttered with numerous tree branches. Flight images of osprey and bald eagles are easier because these two birds frequently fly into uncluttered areas to retrieve nesting material and when hunting prey.

HOTSPOT #47

Spring Creek Ranch

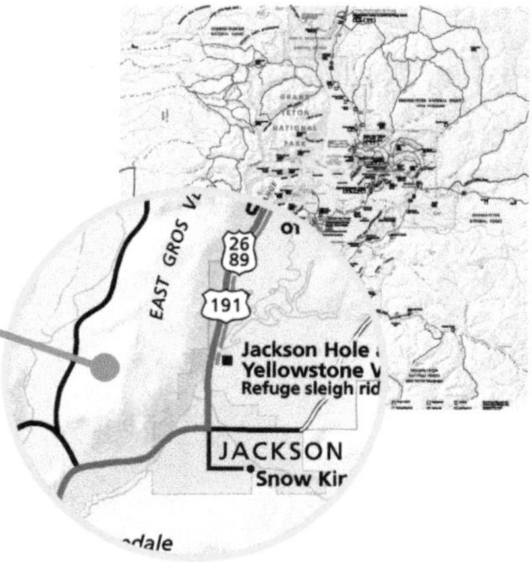

MAP 8

HIGHLIGHTS:

The area from Teton Village to Wyoming 22 bisects residential and ranch areas with wetlands and open meadows. Moose are common in the wetland areas. Elk and foxes are common in the open meadows.

DIRECTIONS

Mileage from Jackson Town Square

From the town square, travel south on Broadway to Highway WY 22, turn right. Continue to the first traffic light and turn right (Spring Gulch Road); the entrance is approximately one mile on the right.

WILDLIFE IN AREA:

East Gros Ventre Butte Wildlife:

Elk and deer are common on the slopes of East Gros Ventre Butte from May through October. They visit the butte to forage the meadows and to have a higher viewpoint on predators. Dusk and dawn are the most common times to see elk; deer are more common during the daytime.

On occasion, badgers are seen near the summit area. Badgers are nocturnal but are occasionally seen during the daytime while raising young in the burrows as additional food is needed. Flickers and other birds are common, especially on the property of Spring Creek Ranch Resort. Much of the butte is private property, so remaining on the public road will be necessary to avoid trespassing.

Site Specific Photography Tips

Many parts of Spring Creek Ranch are private property. However, nice images can be taken from the roadside with lenses in the 100 to 400mm range.

Map #9

COVERING HOTSPOTS #48-50

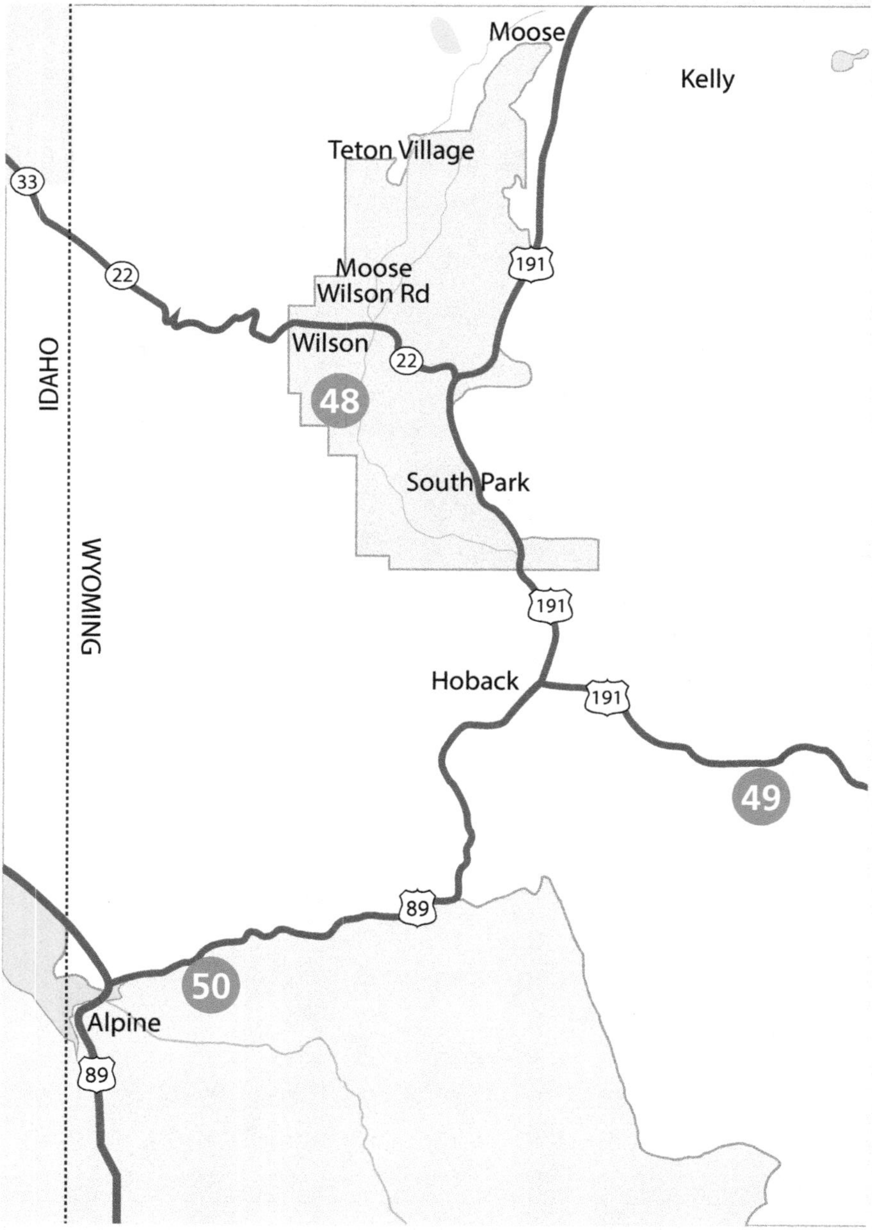

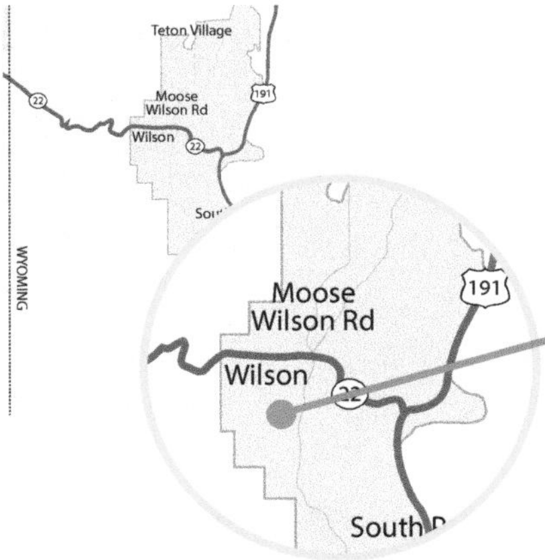

HOTSPOT #48

Boyle's Hill Swan Pond

HIGHLIGHTS:

The swan pond is managed by the Wyoming Wetlands Society to aid in the restoration of Trumpeter Swans belonging to the Rocky Mountain population. Both wild and rehabilitation swans occupy the pond. Canada geese and ducks share the pond with the swans. Moose also frequent the area.

MAP 9

DIRECTIONS

Mileage from Jackson Town Square

Head south from the town square through town to the Maverik Gas Station. Turn right on South Park Loop Road and continue about three miles to the swan pond.

WILDLIFE IN AREA:

Swans and other Waterfowl:

The resident rehabilitation swans do not leave the pond but the wild swans frequently leave in the morning and return in the evenings. The swans are fed daily by the Wyoming Wetlands Society. There is also a bubbler in the pond to provide an ice-free area during the winter. Canada geese and numerous species of ducks also share the pond with the swans.

Moose:

Moose are occasionally seen in the area eating willows.

Site Specific Photography Tips

Waterfowl: The birds commonly swim on the water surface and preen on the banks of the pond. Boyle's Hill is slightly to the northeast providing a nice background for flight shots of the swans, geese or ducks. Lenses in the 400-600mm range are best for waterfowl photography. It is not possible to take low angle photographs because the area surrounding the pond is fenced and restricted.

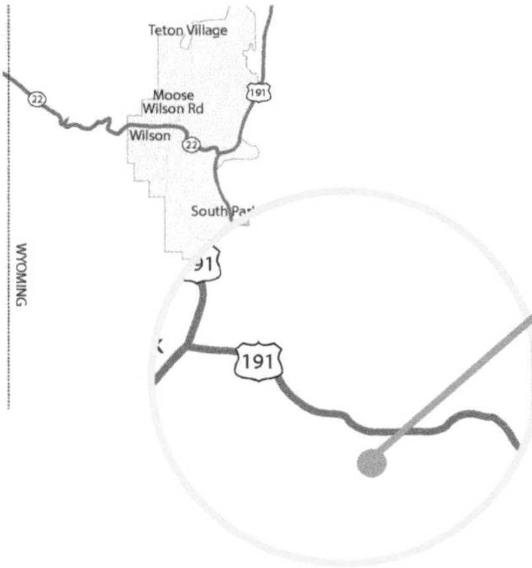

HOTSPOT #49

Hoback Canyon to Granite Hot Springs

HIGHLIGHTS:

Elk are frequently encountered in the stretch from Hoback Junction to a couple miles south of Camp Creek area. Bighorn sheep are frequently seen during the winter months (November through March) near the rocky outcrops and moose are frequent visitors to the Hoback River bottom. Moose are also common along the Granite River to Granite Hot Springs area. When bears first appear from hibernation in April to May, they are occasionally seen near the Camp Creek area and the Hoback River.

DIRECTIONS

Mileage from Jackson Town Square

Travel south on Highway 89 (Broadway) from the town square, approximately 12 miles, to the roundabout at Hoback Junction. Enter roundabout and take the second exit heading toward Pinedale. Hoback Canyon follows the Hoback River to the small town of Bondurant, Wyoming.

WILDLIFE IN AREA:

Elk:

Elk graze the hillsides of Hoback Canyon year-around. From May through October, they are found on the hillsides and in the grassy meadows. Most elk migrate to refugees in winter where they are fed supplements. However, not all elk migrate. During winter, the elk are very easy to spot with their dark bodies against the snowy hillsides.

Bighorn Sheep:

Bighorn sheep are high in the mountains during the summer months and they descend to the lower elevations as the snow accumulates. Sheep are common between November and April near Camp Creek Inn and the rock outcropping just south of the inn.

Moose:

Moose are common year around in the flatter portions of the river valley along the Hoback River. They are also common along Granite Creek leading toward Granite Hot Springs. Moose are often seen bedded down adjacent to the river in winter. They are easy to spot among the leafless deciduous willows with their dark bodies on the white snow.

Site Specific Photography Tips

Elk, Sheep, and Moose: Lenses in the 300-600mm range are best for photographing large animals. These animals generally are not skittish if you give them sufficient space. They are accustomed to vehicles and numerous snowmobiles in the area. Elk will typically be on the hillsides or in the meadows. Moose are among the willows of the river bottom area and sheep will be in the meadows or adjacent to the roadside.

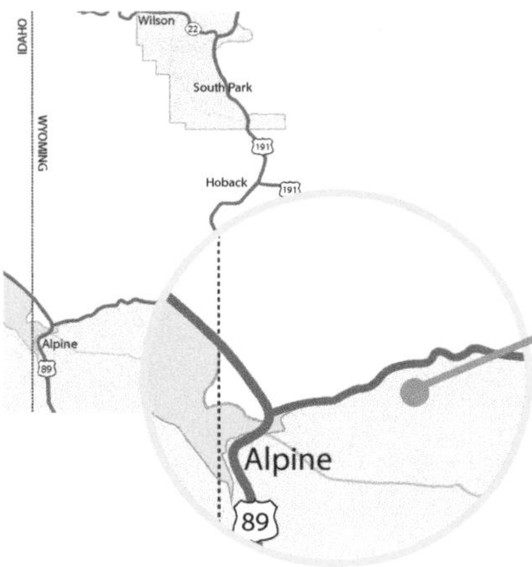

HOTSPOT #50

Snake River Canyon toward Alpine

HIGHLIGHTS:

Elk and mule deer are frequently seen between Hoback Junction and Lunch Counter Kahuna (13.5-30.7 miles), especially in winter, early spring, and late fall. Mountain goats and marmots are common between Lunch Counter and the last turnout before the town of Alpine (31.4-35.9 miles). Moose are occasionally seen in winter near the Nordic Inn (36.3 miles).

DIRECTIONS

Mileage from Jackson Town Square

From Jackson town square, travel south on Highway 89 for 13.5 miles. At Hoback Junction roundabout, take the first exit toward Swan Valley (Highway 89). Travel adjacent to the Snake River past Lunch Counter Kahuna (30.7 miles) and onward to Alpine Junction (36.5 miles).

WILDLIFE IN AREA:

Elk:

There is a winter elk refuge on Fall Creek Road (17.8 miles). Turn left off Highway 89 and travel 0.7 miles. The refuge is on your right just past Dog Creek Ranch. Elk are fed at the refuge from late November roughly through the end of March. The refuge is a restricted area but good photos are possible from outside the front gate.

Mountain Goats:

Mountain goats and marmots are found between Lunch Counter (30.7 miles) and the last turnout before Alpine; the goats live on the canyon hills to the west of the highway. Goats descend the canyon walls and forage the slopes and roadside for grass. On occasion, they are on the east side of the road (Snake River side) but this is rare. The goats are common in winter and less common in spring, summer, and autumn. Use the established pullouts and scope the canyon walls; frequently they are perched on rock ledges or near the roadside.

Marmots:

Yellow-bellied marmots are found between Lunch Counter and the last turnout before Alpine. Marmots live in the rock crevices on the canyon cliffs to the west of the highway. Use established pullouts and scope the canyon walls; frequently they are perched on rock ledges or near the roadside. Marmots hibernate during the winter and emerge from their burrows in late April and return to hibernate in late August. They live among the rocks and descend the canyon walls to forage on grass. Marmots tend to be most active in the sunshine. They will forage by the roadside, though they quickly ascend the canyon walls if you exit your vehicle. The marmots are very common April through August.

Site Specific Photography Tips

Mountain Goats: The mountain goats are relatively tolerant of humans and traffic allowing relatively close images. Telephoto lenses in the 300-600mm range are best. Because the goats are on the rock ledges, frequently your image angle will be upward. To get a more horizontal angle, carefully cross the road of Highway 89 and shoot across to the canyon walls. As the goats move around, diverse backgrounds (blue sky, evergreen trees, snow, etc.) will be possible.

Marmots: These marmots are skittish but can be photographed from your car window using a beanbag or window mount. Lenses in the 400-600mm range are typically best. Make sure to pull completely off the road, as traffic in this area can be dangerous.

Elk: A 500-600mm lens is best for photographing the elk at the refuge. However, a 100-400mm is sufficient when they start the spring migration in April or fall migration in November as they will be near the roadside (Fall Creek Road and Highway 89).

About the Author

Moose Henderson is an award-winning wildlife photographer, scientist, and conservationist. In his youth, he operated a traditional photographic studio doing portraits, weddings, pets, aerials, and commercial/industrial photography. Photographing people was not a passion, so he focused his attention on wild animals. He has photographed wildlife and nature throughout North America, Europe, and Asia. He spent two years in Siberia photographing endangered cranes, storks, and other wildlife.

As a scientist with a doctorate specializing in moose ecology, a master's in wildlife biology, and a bachelor's in environmental geology, he uses his knowledge of animals and animal behavior to capture their true essence. He describes his style of photography as "visceral." Using eye contact, perceived danger, light, color, or atmospheric moods, he seeks to produce images that evoke an emotional response.

His images are distributed by stock agencies (Alamy, Windigo Images, and Getty) with over 11,000 published credits in some of the most prestigious periodicals. Published credits include National Geographic, Smithsonian, Outdoor Photographer, and many others.

Moose lives in the Greater Yellowstone Ecosystem near Jackson, Wyoming. He frequently travels to other locations around North America, Europe, and Asia for dynamic photographic images. Moose is a member of North American Nature Photographers Association (NANPA), Professional Photographers of America (PPA), Art Association of Jackson Hole (AAJH), Teton Photography Group, and the Shoot to Care Campaign for ethical wildlife photography.

Other Books by Sastrugi Press

Cache Creek by Susan Marsh

Five minutes from the hubbub of Jackson's town square, Cache Creek offers the chance for hikers to immerse themselves in wild nature. There is no experience needed: bring attention and a few hours of your time. Cache Creek is a popular hiking, biking, and cross-country ski area on the outskirts of Jackson, Wyoming. It draws dozens to several hundred people per day. Use this unique guide to find your way.

Voices at Twilight by Lori Howe, Ph.D.

Voices at Twilight is a guide takes readers on a visual tour of twelve past and present Wyoming ghost towns. Contained within are travel directions, GPS coordinates, and tips for intrepid readers.

2024 Total Eclipse State Series by Aaron Linsdau

Sastrugi Press has published state-specific guides for the 2024 total eclipse crossing over the United States. Check the Sastrugi Press website for the available state eclipse books:

www.sastrugipress.com/eclipse.

Roaming the Wild by Grover Ratliff

Experience the landscape and wildlife photography of Grover Ratliff in this unique volume. Jackson Hole is home to some of the most iconic landscapes in North America. In this land of harsh winters and short summers, wildlife survives and thrives. People from all around the world travel here to savor the rare vistas of the high Rockies and have the chance to observe bear, moose, and elk. It is an environment like no other, covered in snow most of the year yet blanketed by wildflowers for a few precious months.

Visit Sastrugi Press on the web at www.sastrugipress.com to purchase the above titles in bulk. They are also available from your local bookstore or online retailers in print, e-book, or audiobook form.

Thank you for choosing Sastrugi Press.

"Turn the Page Loose"

MY FIELD NOTES: